NATIONAL DEFENSE RESEARCH INSTITUTE

T0097338

What Works Best When Building Partner Capacity in Challenging Contexts?

Christopher Paul, Jennifer D. P. Moroney, Beth Grill, Colin P. Clarke, Lisa Saum-Manning, Heather Peterson, Brian Gordon

Prepared for the Joint Staff J5, the Office of Cost Assessment and Program Evaluation in the Office of the Secretary of Defense, and the Office of the Under Secretary of Defense for Policy

Approved for public release; distribution unlimited

For more information on this publication, visit www.rand.org/t/rr937

Library of Congress Cataloging-in-Publication Data
ISBN: 978-0-8330-8871-0

Published by the RAND Corporation, Santa Monica, Calif.
© Copyright 2015 RAND Corporation
RAND® is a registered trademark

Cover Image: U.S. Marine Corps photo by MCIPAC Combat Camera Staff Sgt. Jeffrey D. Anderson.

Limited Print and Electronic Distribution Rights

This document and trademark(s) contained herein are protected by law. This representation of RAND intellectual property is provided for noncommercial use only. Unauthorized posting of this publication online is prohibited. Permission is given to duplicate this document for personal use only, as long as it is unaltered and complete. Permission is required from RAND to reproduce, or reuse in another form, any of its research documents for commercial use. For information on reprint and linking permissions, please visit www.rand.org/pubs/permissions.html.

The RAND Corporation is a research organization that develops solutions to public policy challenges to help make communities throughout the world safer and more secure, healthier and more prosperous. RAND is nonprofit, nonpartisan, and committed to the public interest.

RAND's publications do not necessarily reflect the opinions of its research clients and sponsors.

Support RAND
Make a tax-deductible charitable contribution at
www.rand.org/giving/contribute

www.rand.org

Preface

Previous RAND research on effectiveness of U.S. Department of Defense (DoD) efforts to build partner capacity found that several factors that strongly correlated with building partner capacity (BPC) success depend strongly on the partner nation and its context. The obvious conclusion was to recommend that DoD prefer partners with favorable contextual characteristics. Still, circumstances often dictate specific partners regardless of the context. The question remains: When forced to build partner capacity in challenging contexts, what can be done to maximize prospects for success? This report addresses this question.

This research built on previous RAND research and used detailed case studies, analyzed individually and collectively, to provide a foundation of evidence for future resource allocation and policymaking in the specific security cooperation area of BPC.

The findings should be of interest to policymakers and stakeholders in the broader security cooperation arena in the Office of the Secretary of Defense, the regional combatant commands (and the related service components), planners in the departments of Defense and State, and congressional staffs that deal with security assistance to partner nations.

A controlled-access companion annex supports this report with case study details. That annex is available to those with a need to know and appropriate clearances.

Readers may also be interested in the following:

- Christopher Paul, Brian Gordon, Jennifer D. P. Moroney, Lisa Saum-Manning, Beth Grill, Colin P. Clarke, and Heather Peterson, *A Building Partner Capacity Assessment Framework: Tracking Inputs, Outputs, Outcomes, Disrupters, and Workarounds*, Santa Monica, Calif.: RAND Corporation, RR-935-OSD, 2015
- Christopher Paul, Colin P. Clarke, Beth Grill, Stephanie Young, Jennifer D. P. Moroney, Joe Hogler, and Christine Leah, *What Works Best When Building Partner Capacity and Under What Circumstances?* Santa Monica, Calif.: RAND Corporation, MG-1253/1-OSD, 2013
- Christopher Paul, Michael Nixon, Heather Peterson, Beth Grill, and Jessica Yeats, *The RAND Security Cooperation Prioritization and Propensity Matching Tool*, Santa Monica, Calif.: RAND Corporation, TL-112-OSD, 2013

- Jennifer D. P. Moroney, David E. Thaler, and Joe Hogler, *Review of Security Cooperation Mechanisms Combatant Commands Utilize to Build Partner Capacity*, Santa Monica, Calif.: RAND Corporation, RR-413-OSD, 2013.

This research was sponsored jointly by the Joint Staff J5, the Office of Cost Assessment and Program Evaluation in the Office of the Secretary of Defense, and the Office of the Under Secretary of Defense for Policy and was conducted within the International Security and Defense Policy Center of the RAND National Defense Research Institute, a federally funded research and development center sponsored by the Office of the Secretary of Defense, the Joint Staff, the Unified Combatant Commands, the Navy, the Marine Corps, the defense agencies, and the defense Intelligence Community under contract W91WAW-12-C-0030.

For more information on the RAND International Security and Defense Policy Center, see http://www.rand.org/nsrd/ndri/centers/isdp.html or contact the director (contact information is provided on the web page).

Contents

Figures and Tables

Figures

Tables

Summary

Previous RAND research used case studies of building partner capacity (BPC) in 29 countries over two decades to identify factors correlated with BPC success.[1] That study found nine factors highly correlated with success: four under U.S. control, four inherent in the partner nation (PN) or under its control, and one jointly determined between the United States and the PN. That report recommended that the U.S. Department of Defense (DoD) increase the consistency with which favorable factors under U.S. control are applied to BPC efforts and also recommended giving preference, when possible, to partners likely to have favorable characteristics. However, strategic imperatives sometimes compel the United States to work with PNs that lack these favorable factors but with which the United States needs to conduct BPC anyway. This report addresses the question implicit in that observation: When forced to conduct BPC in challenging contexts (that is, contexts lacking characteristics correlated with BPC success), what can be done to maximize prospects for success? This report addresses this question.

Methods and Approach

To answer that question, we relied on four deep-dive case studies of carefully selected PNs in which U.S. BPC efforts faced a host of contextual challenges. These deep-dive case studies included extensive review of available reports and documentation and interviews across a wide range of stakeholders, including current and former officials in the embassies, the Office of the Secretary of Defense, and the Joint Staff and combatant command, service component command, interagency, and relevant security cooperation program office representatives. Concurrent with the deep-dive case studies, we also developed a logic model for BPC using a process that involved both deductive and inductive input.[2] The resulting logic model contains not only the logical chain of

---

[1]   Christopher Paul, Colin P. Clarke, Beth Grill, Stephanie Young, Jennifer D. P. Moroney, Joe Hogler, and Christine Leah, *What Works Best When Building Partner Capacity and Under What Circumstances?* Santa Monica, Calif.: RAND Corporation, MG-1253/1-OSD, 2013.

[2]   A companion report describes this model: Christopher Paul, Brian Gordon, Jennifer D. P. Moroney, Lisa Saum-Manning, Beth Grill, Colin P. Clarke, and Heather Peterson, *A Building Partner Capacity Assessment*

inputs, activities, outputs, and outcomes traditional of logic models but also includes "disrupters," the things that can interfere with the conversion of inputs to outputs or of outputs to outcomes. This list of potential disrupters should be particularly useful to those planning BPC in challenging contexts because it includes specific ways that contextual challenges can interfere with BPC functioning. The disrupters are presented in 15 different categories:

- objectives and goals
- U.S. internal contention
- U.S. continuity and agility
- U.S. trainers
- U.S.-PN relationships
- curriculum and training materials
- equipment mismatch
- sustainment
- corruption or governance
- human rights violations and restrictions
- security situation
- PN willingness to support or conduct BPC
- PN willingness to organize for increased capacity
- PN personnel and trainees
- PN infrastructure, facilities, and logistics.

The logic model also lists possible workarounds for the identified disrupters, although contextually specific solutions may be preferred in any given situation.

Variations in How Contextual Challenges Play Out

Challenges and disrupters can be considered based on variation on a temporal dimension (before, during, and after an event), across different levels (strategic, operational, and tactical), and by origin (United States or PN). The logic model and the associated disrupters cover three different temporal phases of BPC. The preengagement phase, when plans are made and inputs are prepared; the engagement phase, when training and equipment are delivered, exercises take place, etc.; and the postengagement phase, when trained troops are (or are not) formed into units and mobilized for intended purposes and equipment received is (or is not) distributed and used for operations.

In addition to variations in timing of the effects of challenges or disrupters, they can also occur at different levels. We identified three levels, which correspond roughly

---

Framework: Tracking Inputs, Outputs, Outcomes, Disrupters, and Workarounds, Santa Monica, Calif.: RAND Corporation, RR-935-OSD, 2015.

to the strategic, operational, and tactical levels (the doctrinal three levels of war). At what we are equating with the strategic level, challenges came from the most senior leadership within the PN government or the PN military or were inherent in the PN's economy or national security objectives. An example would be a PN's president deciding to terminate visas for all U.S. trainers because of failed negotiations in another aspect of foreign policy. At the equivalent to the operational level, disrupters concerned PN military services, the commanders of formations of PN troops or bases, or bases themselves. For example, a commander may decide not to allow his unit to participate in the training or may insist on different training than what was planned or agreed to. The lowest level, which we equate to the tactical level, included the interactions between trainees and trainers, the details of facilities, or small-scale logistics. Examples would be inadequacies in the level of motivation of the troops in training, their level of preparation for training, or the condition of their gear. Challenges can play out at multiple levels simultaneously: The level of preparation of training troops creates a tactical concern for trainers but may have resulted from a strategic- or operational-level decision not to send troops that were better prepared to participate.

A final dimension of variation is in the origins of challenges or disrupters. While the default assumption is that many contextual challenges are brought to that context by deficiencies in the PN's government, economy, military, or security situation, it was clear in the case studies that some significant challenges were brought to the context by the United States rather than by the PN. Certain complexities and weaknesses are inherent in how the United States is organized and authorized to conduct BPC, and there are certain vulnerabilities in execution. When categorizing challenges and disrupters, it is also important to note the partner originating the challenge. Taking these three categories together creates a useful framework for better understanding disrupters and challenges and, more importantly, for identifying opportunities to make improvements.

Conclusions and Results

We reached several important findings regarding BPC success when working with partners in challenging contexts:

- Many challenges stem from shortcomings in U.S. policy or practice.
- Lack of partner willingness, if present, is a particularly critical challenge.
- Agreement within and between the United States and the PN on objectives and approaches is key for success.
- Progress with partners in challenging contexts can be highly dependent on the personalities and capabilities of individual PN counterparts.
- PN ministerial capacity can be extremely important.

When working with robust partners, the partner usually fills gaps in U.S. processes or support. However, a PN that already faces a number of contextual challenges often lacks the means to cover gaps in U.S. support. To offer an analogy, **when the United States drops the ball with a robust partner, the partner usually picks it up; when the United States drops the ball with a partner in an already challenging context, the ball falls.**

While partners in challenging contexts often lack the ability to fill gaps in U.S. processes, the PN remains critical to effective BPC. Specifically, **the lack of willingness to support and participate in BPC of PN personnel at any level (head of state or ministry, service or command, or individual trainees) can disrupt BPC efforts.** Further, such willingness is often contingent on a shared understanding of and agreement on both the approach to and the goals of BPC efforts.

Finally, a partner's ministerial capacity (that is, the size, health, and capability of its ministry of defense or equivalent) plays a significant role in both managing the BPC process from the partner's side and in prospects for organizing for and funding the sustainment of built capacity. **When capacity built through U.S. BPC efforts has endured rather than atrophied rapidly, an effective PN ministry has played a role in that outcome.**

Factors found to be correlated with success in BPC more broadly also proved to be important when working with partners in challenging contexts. Previous research found nine factors correlated with BPC success (four under U.S. control, four inherent to or under the control of the PN, and one joint between the United States and the PN).[3] Eight of these nine were firmly validated in these analyses:[4]

- consistency in both the funding and implementation of these initiatives
- matching BPC efforts with PN objectives and absorptive capacity
- including a sustainment component in the initiatives
- the PN investing its own funds to support or sustain capacity
- the PN having sufficient absorptive capacity
- the PN having high governance indicators
- the PN having a strong economy
- the PN sharing security interests with the United States.

Comparative analyses of the case studies emphasized two of these validated results in particular. First, **consistency is key—not just consistent funding but also consistent objectives, consistent agreements, and consistent relationships.** The narratives

---

[3] Paul, Clarke, et al., 2013.

[4] The one factor that was *not* supported was "spending more money on BPC or undertaking more BPC initiative." In general, and certainly with diminishing returns, more spending gets more BPC. However, in challenging contexts, this correlation did not hold up, with spending in excess resulting only in waste, fuel for corruption, and other inefficiencies.

of the cases considered highlight numerous instances in which inconsistency damaged BPC efforts. These included not only delays in funding and unnecessary changes to already effective delivery in progress but also changing or conflicting goals or mission scope; changes in the levels at which the PN was being engaged (abandoning effectively engaged counterparts); and, perhaps most grievous in the eyes of PN officials, reneging on agreements. In contrast, the case studies revealed progress and success when consistency was maintained. Consistent relationships and training with a specific unit and its officers resulted in notable increases in capacity over time; long-term relationships, even if the U.S. counterpart changed, led to increased mutual respect, more-effective engagement, and greater support for BPC on the PN side.

Second, **without attention to sustainment and maintenance, capacity atrophies**. Without attention to the sustainment of capabilities (including refresher training for troops and maintenance of facilities and equipment), they quickly begin to degrade. Troops lose proficiency; units lose proficiency more rapidly as individuals transfer to different units or leave the military (routine personnel processes). Without institutionalizing training (or a robust and ongoing train-the-trainer program), such atrophy is unavoidable. The cases revealed even worse levels of decay on the maintenance side. Most of the studied militaries lacked any kind of culture of, or training for, maintenance. Even when PN forces were willing to conduct maintenance, lack of training, tools, and parts specific to the equipment provided in BPC efforts doomed that equipment. Road vehicles were used until they stopped, then abandoned by the roadside. Numbers of aircraft and boats slowly dwindled; some failed and were then cannibalized in the hope of repairing remaining craft. Short-term successes turned into long-term failure as developed or improved capabilities trended back toward the baseline.

Recommendations

These findings (and the findings of previous RAND research) suggest the following recommendations:

- First, get your own house in order:
    - **BPC planners should engage senior leaders and resource managers in every stage of the planning cycle, from concept to evaluation, to ensure that aspects under U.S. control are well coordinated and conducted.** Weaknesses in delivery or coordination are magnified when the partner context contains additional challenges. Effective coordination may require senior leader attention, vigorous engagement with the bureaucracy and mobilizing of stakeholders, and carefully stitching together a patchwork of authorities and mechanisms. Attendance at security cooperation–focused conferences can help

establish networks to enable coordination; establishing and committing to regular interagency monitoring and evaluation focus groups is another possible contributor.

— **Ask Congress to reform existing BPC mechanisms to increase responsiveness, simplify processes, allow for sustainment, and strengthen spending control.**[5] While some of the hard work of aligning and coordinating U.S. efforts falls on those who plan, manage, and execute such efforts, some of the existing authorities and regulations place undue burdens on those involved in this process. **Specifically, existing mechanisms either need to be broadened to support a wider range of efforts over a longer period or need to be joined by (or replaced by) new authorities and programs able to resource sustainment in later years.**

— **Increase the options for agility available to managers and executors, both to respond to changes on the ground and to incentivize or disincentivize PN behaviors, as needed.** Errors made elsewhere in the BPC patchwork bureaucracy would be less critical if they could be corrected easily further down the chain; this is particularly true for decisions on equipment or materiel. Increased funding flexibility would allow those delivering BPC to reallocate funds to solve emergent problems and save otherwise failing engagements or events. Better coordination across the bureaucracy could increase agility: First, if U.S. government stakeholders are engaged at all levels of planning, senior leaders can delegate authority more easily; second, if executors have networked effectively, even if they themselves do not have control or authority over certain resource flows, they may know (and be on good terms with) the office that does.

• Second, anticipate challenges and plan accordingly:

— **Include assessment considerations in the planning process.** Planning should include not only preliminary assessments of likely challenges but also the collection of assessment data throughout the process. Much valuable assessment information can be collected informally from subject-matter experts, but some will require more-rigorous data-collection efforts, and these should be identified and put in place during the planning phase. Something specific that can support assessment is to stipulate assessment (and related data collection) as part of the orders and contracts involved in the execution of BPC. Finally, the planning phase is an opportunity to make sure the BPC objectives are specific, measurable, achievable, results oriented, and time-bound. If they are not, both planning and later assessment will suffer.

---

[5]   Also recommended in Jennifer D. P. Moroney, David E. Thaler, and Joe Hogler, *Review of Security Cooperation Mechanisms Combatant Commands Utilize to Build Partner Capacity*, Santa Monica, Calif.: RAND Corporation, RR-413-OSD, 2013.

- **Survey likely challenges at the outset of an effort.** During planning and prior to events (particularly exercises or training events), planners should assess and document the likelihood of possible challenges and disrupters (perhaps holistically, using a framework similar to the one proposed here). Areas identified as possible trouble spots should be scrutinized with greater intensity (either additional subject-matter expert input or formal data collection).
  - **Anticipate challenges and plan workarounds.** Once likely challenges have been identified, prioritize the elimination or amelioration of those most likely to seriously disrupt the effort. When possible, preventive workarounds should be put in place to decrease the likelihood of high-threat disruptions. When prevention is not feasible, plans should include branches and sequels, should possible disruptions emerge. To support such efforts, maintain constant vigilance for emergent challenges and disrupters, so they can be fixed or worked around as soon as possible. Contingency plans should be prepared in case the worst possible challenges materialize and cannot be mitigated, and PN officials should be warned of possible threats to successful collaboration.
- Third, match delivery plans to the partner's willingness, interests, and absorption capacity:
  - Because effective BPC matches what the partner wants and is actually capable of using, **strive to reach shared BPC objectives with the PN.** Having concordant objectives, documented at a level of specificity that enables collaborative planning, is critical. Sharing objectives is relatively straightforward when there are substantial overlaps between U.S. and PN security interests, but when these diverge, some kind of agreement on objectives must be found. When the United States and the PN have different priorities, some kind of compromise or quid pro quo may be required. At a minimum, U.S. officials should understand where key objectives diverge with the PN's, and this understanding should be shared widely, especially with those regularly engaging with the PN (executors and BPC deliverers). For example, if the United States wants to build capacity to resolve one kind of security threat but the PN's threat priorities lie elsewhere (as is often the case), it would likely be better to reach an agreement about the balance of where built capabilities will be used from the outset (perhaps one for one, with one trained formation addressing the primary U.S. concern, and one sent to address the primary PN concern) rather than risk the PN either using all new capabilities for its top priority or being less motivated to participate because the BPC does not at all help with the PN's top priority.
  - **Match equipment to partners, both in terms of what they can use and what they can maintain.** Too often, equipment provided through BPC is ill-suited to PN forces because it is either too sophisticated for their use, ill-suited to their environment or terrain, or beyond their capability (or inclination) to maintain. Detailed surveys of the equipment and maintenance capabilities the

partner already has and an understanding of the maintenance required for the equipment the United States proposes to provide should underpin this process. Make sure that equipment choices are based on what works for the PN, not what is most convenient for the United States.

- Fourth, plan for sustainment:
  - **Plan for sustainment in discussions with U.S. stakeholders.** Related to the need to match equipment to partners is the need to plan for sustainment of capabilities. A complete sustainment plan will recognize what ongoing inputs and activities will need to take place to sustain trained and equipped forces. This includes ongoing funding, refresher or extended training, replacement equipment, spare parts, maintenance skills, and maintenance activities. The sustainment plan should include details about where these inputs will come from and who will conduct the needed activities.
  - **Examine ministerial-level capacity from the outset.** Sustainment issues must be considered from a strategic standpoint as well. In some cases, U.S. BPC efforts have focused on the operational and tactical levels first, only to determine later that the PN lacked the funding, manpower, and other resources needed to sustain the capacity built in the long term. Such an ad hoc approach will make it difficult to build on current, much less past, success.
- Fifth, strive for consistency but retain agility:
  - **Be agile.** Mentioned above is the need for more-flexible authorities, but BPC in a challenging context, with or without revised authorities, requires agility in planning and execution. Specifically, at the level of execution, be willing to work with PN elements that are willing (and able) to work with you. Especially where PN willingness is limited, working with a less-attractive but interested PN formation can allow an initial success, which can create momentum and incentives for other PN units to become more cooperative.
  - Struggling BPC is characterized by fits and starts, moving targets, interrupted funding and delivery, and constantly changing points of contact. When managing and executing BPC, **strive for consistency over time in terms of objectives, funding, and plans** to the extent possible. At every level of the BPC bureaucracy, envision and execute based on a cumulative "building block" approach, rather than constantly beginning anew. Minor adjustments to make something work better can preserve existing successes and build cumulatively toward reaching objectives and goals. Consistency over time requires a long-term view.

Acknowledgments

We are indebted to our thoughtful and engaged sponsor points of contact, David Lowe and Louise Hoehl in the Office of Cost Assessment and Program Evaluation in the Office of the Secretary of Defense (OSD/CAPE), Maureen Bannon and Aaron Jay in the Office of the Under Secretary of Defense for Policy (OUSD[P]), and CAPT John Sniegowski and Sarah Braswell in the Joint Staff J5. Their guidance and support were instrumental in the development and dissemination of this report and its findings. We also owe debts of gratitude to several other DoD personnel who supported earlier research in this area, attended interim briefings, commented on draft slides, or otherwise provided valuable feedback on the research: Timothy Bright, Tom Johnson, and Melissa Kirkner of OSD/CAPE; James Miner of the Defense Security Cooperation Agency; and CAPT Connie Frizzell and CDR John Mann of the Joint Staff J5.

We thank several of our RAND colleagues who offered engaging discussion on this topic, foundational insights, or comments on draft materials: Seth Jones, Terry Kelly, Thomas Szayna, Michael McNerney, and Jan Osburg. Joe Hogler, RAND adjunct staff, was instrumental in arranging and supporting interviews for one of our deep-dive case studies. RAND administrative assistant Maria Falvo, editor Phyllis Gilmore, and production editor Beth Bernstein contributed substantially to the form and fettle of the final product, as did the two scholars who reviewed this document as part of the RAND quality assurance process: Christopher Schnaubelt and James Schear.

Finally, we thank all the personnel in OSD, at the combatant commands, in the components, in the embassies and military groups, and elsewhere who took the time to share information and insights about BPC in the specific country cases. We refrain from thanking you all by name to keep the terms of our anonymous interviews, but you know who you are, and we appreciate your contributions.

Abbreviations

AOR	area of responsibility
AWOL	absent without leave
BPC	building partner capacity
CCMD	combatant command
DoD	U.S. Department of Defense
FP	force protection
OPTEMPO	operational tempo
OSD/CAPE	Office of Cost Assessment and Program Evaluation in the Office of the Secretary of Defense
OUSD[P]	Office of the Under Secretary of Defense for Policy
PN	partner nation
POI	program of instruction
SMART	specific, measurable, attainable, results oriented, and time bound
SOF	special operations forces

CHAPTER ONE

Introduction

Security cooperation has long been an important instrument of the U.S. government and the U.S. Department of Defense (DoD) for advancing national security objectives by, with, and through allies and partner countries, including building critical relationships; securing peacetime and contingency access; and building partner capacity (BPC), the focus of this report. Previous RAND research used case studies of BPC in 29 countries over two decades to identify factors correlated with BPC success.[1] That study found nine factors highly correlated with success: four under U.S. control, four inherent in the partner nation (PN) or under its control, and one jointly determined between the United States and the PN (all are listed in the next chapter). That study recommended that DoD increase the consistency with which favorable factors under U.S. control are applied to BPC efforts and also recommended giving preference, when possible, to partners likely to have favorable characteristics. The key phrase there is, of course, "where possible." We recognize that strategic imperatives sometimes compel the United States to work with PNs that lack these favorable factors but with which the United States needs to succeed at BPC anyway. The question remains: When forced to conduct BPC in challenging contexts (that is, contexts lacking characteristics correlated with BPC success), what can be done to maximize prospects for positive outcomes? This report addresses this question.

Methods and Approach

The goal of this research was to identify paths to successful BPC when circumstances require working in challenging contexts. The identification of such paths requires both a nuanced understanding of the contextual challenges and how they play out during BPC efforts and an understanding of different strategies for minimizing the impact of, or working around, these challenges.

---

[1] Christopher Paul, Colin P. Clarke, Beth Grill, Stephanie Young, Jennifer D. P. Moroney, Joe Hogler, and Christine Leah, *What Works Best When Building Partner Capacity and Under What Circumstances?* Santa Monica, Calif.: RAND Corporation, MG-1253/1-OSD, 2013.

Logic Model Basics

We have chosen to use a logic model to capture the elements and connections required in BPC, one that "describes how the activities, resources, and contextual factors work together to achieve the intended outcome."[2] We chose to use the language of logic models here to structure our discussion of how and where contextual challenges affect the logic of BPC and to highlight possible ways to minimize or avoid adverse effects (how BPC can still succeed in challenging contexts).

Logic models traditionally include effort inputs, outputs, and outcomes. Some styles of logic model development also report activities and effects. Figure 1.1 presents these elements in sequence.

Inputs, Activities, Outputs, Outcomes, and Impacts

The *inputs* to a program or effort are the resources required to conduct the program. These will, of course, include personnel and funding but can also include guidance, agreements, authorities, and plans. Inputs are usually more specific than the listed general categories, perhaps indicating specific expertise required, numbers of personnel (or person hours or effort available), etc. An effort's *activities* are the verbs associated with the use of the inputs and are the undertakings of the program; these might include transporting and delivering equipment or gathering together instructions, curriculum, and trainees within training facilities to deliver training. Activities involve the use of inputs to create outputs. In fact, some logic model templates omit activities because these just connect inputs to outputs and can often be inferred by imagining what has to be done with the inputs to generate the outputs.

The *outputs* are what conducting the activities with the inputs produces. Outputs include traditional measures of performance and indicators that the activities have been executed as planned. These might, for example, include execution records, attendance records, and course completion rates. *Outcomes* (or effects) are "the state . . .

Figure 1.1
Logic Model Template

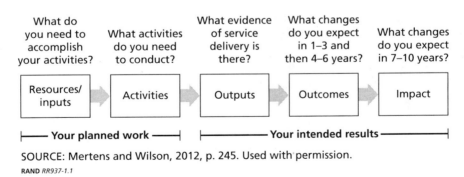

SOURCE: Mertens and Wilson, 2012, p. 245. Used with permission.
RAND RR937-1.1

---

2   Donna M. Mertens and Amy T. Wilson, *Program Evaluation Theory and Practice: A Comprehensive Guide*, New York: The Guilford Press, 2012, p. 244.

a program is expected to have changed."[3] This is the result of the overall process: The inputs resource the activities, and the activities produce the outputs. The outputs lead to the outcomes. Outcomes are characteristics or behaviors of the recipients, not of the program or effort. The outputs are related to the program or effort and describe the products or services the program provides. Outcomes are the results (or lack of results) of the outputs produced, not just their delivery or receipt.[4]

The *impact* of a program or effort is the expected cumulative, long-term, or enduring contribution. There is no clear dividing line between immediate- and short-term outcomes, medium-term outcomes, and long-term impacts. In fact, impact is beyond the scope of the BPC portion of the activities in many cases, being part of the broader security cooperation or even foreign policy objectives.

Constraints, Barriers, Disrupters, and Unintended Consequences

In addition to specifying inputs, activities, outputs, outcomes, and impacts, logic modeling provides an opportunity to think about things that might go wrong. Which assumptions are the most vulnerable? Which of the inputs are most likely to be late? Which of the activities might the adversary disrupt or are contingent on the weather? How can various contextual challenges explicitly affect the subprocesses of the overall BPC effort? These things can be listed as part of the logic model, placed next to (or between) the nodes they might disrupt. For example, if local contractors might abscond with funds allocated for training facility maintenance or if they are vulnerable to weather that can wash out roads and prevent them from arriving to complete their contracts, these things could be noted between the relevant input and activity. If PN posttraining personnel assignment policies can prevent the translation of an output (certified trainees) into a longer-term outcome (formed units), it could be noted between outputs and outcomes. For example, heavy attrition was a major obstacle to U.S. efforts to bolster security forces in Afghanistan. The Office of the Inspector General for Afghanistan Reconstruction noted in 2010 that the Afghan National Army's AWOL rate was 12 percent. These losses, coupled with high levels of approved absence and frequent reassignments, left many units with insufficient personnel to permit effective operations.[5]

Barriers (disrupters) do not necessarily completely disrupt processes (although some do), but all will at least slow down or diminish the rate of success, the rate (or efficiency) of conversion of inputs into outputs or of outputs into outcomes. Perhaps they are best conceived as being like the coefficient of friction in physics. A severe

---

[3] Peter H. Rossi, Mark W. Lipsey, and Howard E. Freeman, *Evaluation: A Systematic Approach*, Thousand Oaks, Calif.: Sage Publications, 2004, p. 204.

[4] Rossi, Lipsey, and Freeman, 2004.

[5] Office of the Special Inspector General for Afghanistan Reconstruction, "Actions Needed to Improve the Reliability of Afghan Security Force Assessments," June 29, 2010.

enough disrupter has a coefficient of 1, wholly precluding progress past it (a barrier); a lesser disrupter might have a coefficient of 0.2, causing just 20-percent inefficiency in the conversion of an input to an output. Depending on the context, 20-percent inefficiency may be acceptable.

One of the most common sources of friction in challenging contexts is corruption within PN bureaucracies. Equipment is sold on black markets instead of reaching its intended destination; customs agents seize portions of shipments in the name of unofficial "taxes"; and military leaders divert resources for personal gain. Corruption rarely causes the loss of all equipment or resources but does dramatically decrease the efficiency and throughput of inputs. For example, in Peru, the arrest of a notorious drug trafficker nicknamed "El Vaticano" and his relationship with Peru's head of intelligence, Vlad Montesinos, illustrated how disastrous corruption was for attempts to build PN counternarcotics capability in Peru.[6]

Workarounds

Where disrupters are present (and when working in challenging contexts, it is a safe bet that they are), how might the integrity of the logic model be preserved? Workarounds might include simply putting more of an input or activity in place, realizing that a certain amount is being lost to "friction" (i.e., train more personnel than there are billets in anticipation of some level of attrition) or identifying some new activity or effort to minimize or remove the effects of the disrupter (i.e., identify alternative sources of funding to reduce the negative effects of other funding restrictions). If a logic model includes possible disrupters, it can also include possible workarounds. Effective workarounds for common disrupters are an important aspect of efforts to identify what works best when conducting BPC in challenging contexts.

Deductive and Inductive Contributions to Identifying Disrupters and Workarounds

To develop a logic model for BPC, we sought to populate inputs, activities, outputs, outcomes, disrupters (between each of the other categories of elements), and possible workarounds or solutions for those disrupters. We approached the identification and refinement of logic model elements and their connections in two ways: deductively and inductively. First, we began to model deductively, from the top down, in an abstract way based on our experience and research on BPC, existing guidance, the extensive literature on the subject, and common sense and logic. Second, we sought inductive input from case studies. We built provisional logic models for the BPC efforts conducted in four cases (case selection is described later in the chapter). These case-specific logic models captured specific inputs, outputs, and disrupters that were important in the specific cases. The synthesis of four case-specific logic models with the broader, deductively based logic model led to our initial BPC training and equipping logic

---

[6]   Vanda Felbab-Brown, *Shooting Up: Counterinsurgency and the War on Drugs*, Washington, D.C.: Brookings Institution Press, 2009, p. 59.

model. This model was further refined (and demonstrated to be applicable) in the context of the specific cases.

In the presentation of challenging context disrupters in Chapter Three, we note which actually occurred in the empirical cases considered and which are just possible disrupters (from our experience with other cases or as logical possibilities). Similarly, the discussion of workarounds indicates which have proven effective in the actual cases. This serves as a form of empirical validation of these disrupters and workarounds beyond what was required to enter the logic model.

We also drew lessons from the rich narrative details of each of the deep-dive case studies.

Case Selection

Case selection for these analyses was bounded by a number of constraints and preferences. Some of these constraints were not particularly methodological but had to do with resource constraints and stakeholder equities. Other constraints were methodological and ensured sound analyses. Case-selection constraints included the following:

- **There should be three to six cases.** Previous experience conducting case study analyses of U.S. BPC efforts showed that such cases are usually both complicated and poorly documented.[7] Completing case data collection to the desired depth with the resources available would thus limit the number of cases we could examine.
- **All cases need to be instances of BPC within challenging contexts.** We wanted to be sure that all the selected cases did, in fact, include the kinds of contextual challenges of interest for these analyses. We were aware that worldwide data for some countries might indicate that suboptimalities and challenges were likely to be present but were not actually present.
- **Outcomes need to vary.** Of the cases, some needed to be more and some less successful (or to have more and less successful aspects) so that we could observe the relationships between other factors and outcomes. Differences in outcome could be within a case (a case in which early efforts failed, but later efforts were more successful, or a case with multiple lines of effort with different levels of success) or between cases.
- **The cases need to involve significant levels of U.S. BPC engagement.** In addition to cases that included contextual challenges, we wanted to be able to examine efforts to conduct BPC while facing the challenges. This required some level of U.S. BPC engagement. Further, greater effort would provide more data points, so we favored a significant level of BPC engagement by considering only countries in the top half of annual U.S. BPC spending volume.

---

[7] See, for example Paul, Clarke, et al., 2013.

- **The cases need to include some history of U.S. BPC engagement.** Similarly, we sought cases in which the United States had been conducting BPC for some time, so that it would be possible (and meaningful) to consider its level of success. Countries that have only recently become the object of significant BPC efforts would have been less useful.
- **The cases need to cross multiple BPC objective areas.** We sought cases in which BPC efforts spanned more than one BPC objective area.[8] Having multiple objective areas in a case would allow the United States to see whether challenging contexts have differing influence in different BPC areas. Further, having multiple BPC objective areas available would allow us to develop and test assessment frameworks applicable across areas.
- **The cases should have BPC objective areas in common.** Inasmuch as having multiple BPC objective areas available has analytic benefits, having one or more BPC objective areas common to one or more cases would be useful for discerning whether observed differences are due to differences in contextual challenges, other differences in context, or differences in BPC due to different objective areas.
- **In no case should "relationship building" have been a primary BPC objective area.** As we have noted elsewhere,[9] there is an important qualitative difference when BPC is done primarily to build relationships or gain access as opposed to being conducted with a primary goal of actually building capacity. While relationship building is an important part of foreign policy and security cooperation more broadly, we preferred cases focused primarily on capacity building when developing assessment methods and identifying effective practices within challenging contexts.
- **Multiple combatant command (CCMD) areas of responsibility (AORs) should be represented.** To be broadly representative of the kinds of context in which the United States conducts BPC and to be inclusive of multiple CCMD stakeholders in the research process, we sought to include cases from multiple CCMD AORs.

---

[8] We were aware that BPC takes different forms and is used to pursue a range of different activities. In Paul, Clarke, et al., 2013, we synthesized the wide range of goals that BPC is used to pursue into six BPC objective areas: five capacity-building objectives and a sixth objective that was a foreign policy objective that is pursued through BPC efforts (labeled "A" below to indicate its qualitative difference from 1 to 5):

1. internal security, including counterinsurgency, counterterrorism, and forces for counternarcotics
2. conventional forces for self-defense and regional security, including air and missile defense and coalition operations
3. specialty forces for external use, including counterterrorism, peacekeeping, peace enforcement, humanitarian assistance, reconstruction, other stability operations, counterpiracy, and counternarcotics
4. ministerial capacity, defense institution creation, and reform
5. border security, along with maritime security, counterpiracy, countertrafficking, and crop eradication
A. relationship building or maintenance and securing access.

[9] Paul, Clarke, et al., 2013.

To identify case candidates that jointly met these criteria, we began with data already available to RAND. We considered 29 cases studied in previous research to form a preliminary list.[10] DoD considers the specific cases discussed (both candidates throughout the selection process and those ultimately selected) to be sensitive, and they are thus are not listed anywhere in this report; interested parties are referred to the restricted-access companion report mentioned in the preface. Examples are used throughout this report but are drawn from cases with which the authors are familiar, including those outside the 29 studied in previous research and the four studied in detail in support of this effort. Readers should *not* assume that cases mentioned by name are necessarily cases selected as part of this process and studied specifically for this project.

In addition to the 29 cases for which we already had substantial data, we drew on global data from other RAND research to identify countries with low propensity for BPC success.[11] Of the 29 cases with which we began, 13 did not have relationship building or access as a primary BPC objective *and* were in the bottom half of BPC overall propensity scores (a first-cut proxy for having challenging contextual features) and so qualified as initial candidates.

We also prepared a list of all countries in the bottom half of overall BPC propensity scores. We reviewed this list jointly with sponsors to make sure we were considering other cases of potential interest (additional cases from underrepresented CCMDs or cases that were prominent in recent discussions inside sponsor organizations and the United States that might serve other interests if studied). This review led to the addition of eight candidate cases to our existing list of 13.

Using this list of 21 initial candidates, we began preliminary data collection to ascertain which group of cases best met the selection criteria. A review of the BPC funding history for all candidates quickly revealed that efforts in four of the candidates were too nascent to satisfy that criterion, for example. After compiling preliminary data and reviewing results, we identified (in concert with the sponsor) eight cases as serious candidates that appeared to meet all selection criteria.

We then collected additional data on each of these eight cases for a viability review prior to making final case selections. Four of the eight cases were confirmed as strong candidates (additional data collection validated their satisfaction of individual case criteria, and as a set, they adequately satisfied collective case criteria). With the sponsors' concurrence, we elected to move forward to deep-dive case study data collection and analysis for these four cases.

---

[10] Paul, Clarke, et al., 2013.

[11] Christopher Paul, Michael Nixon, Heather Peterson, Beth Grill, and Jessica Yeats, *The RAND Security Cooperation Prioritization and Propensity Matching Tool*, Santa Monica, Calif.: RAND Corporation, TL-112-OSD, 2013.

The four selected cases satisfy all the case-selection criteria. All were confirmed as cases of BPC in challenging contexts; there was variation in level of success of BPC efforts, both within and between cases; all had significant histories of significant BPC engagement; the four cases came from four different CCMD AORs; and the cases included three different BPC objective areas (all four cases included BPC for border security or maritime forces; all four cases included ministerial capacity building; and three of them included BPC for forces for internal security).

These four cases are not "statistically" representative (that is, they were not randomly selected from a specified population, and the probability that they might have been selected from such a population cannot be meaningfully quantified). However, they were chosen in accordance with a reasonable set of criteria and are intended to be broadly representative of a range of BPC activities and a range of contextual challenges that such activities might face. While confidence in the generalizability of findings based on these cases cannot be precisely quantified, results make sense intuitively, correspond with the authors' collective experience with BPC, and are likely to hold across a wide range of similar efforts and contexts.

Outline of the Remainder of the Report

Chapter Two presents insights, observations, and conclusions regarding the conduct of BPC in challenging contexts and are based on comparative analyses of four deep-dive case studies. Chapter Three lists and describes the contextual challenges, disrupters, and workarounds identified in this project and presents them in a way that should be useful for planning for future BPC efforts or for process improvement for ongoing or completed BPC efforts. Chapter Four concludes with summary recommendations based on the analyses in the previous chapters. The appendix repeats the disrupters presented in Chapter Three in a single table.

CHAPTER TWO

Insights from Building Partner Capacity in Four Contextually Challenging Cases

As detailed in Chapter One, this effort included deep-dive case studies of BPC efforts that faced a range of contextual challenges in four different PNs. This chapter makes general observations and draws useful insights from the consideration of these four cases collectively and in comparison with each other.

Results from a Previous Study Largely Validated in the New Case Studies

A previous study used comparative analyses of two decades of case study data for 29 partners to identify effective BPC practices and contextual requirements or barriers.[1] The study found nine factors correlated with BPC success—four under U.S. control, four inherent to or under the control of the PN, and one joint between the United States and the PN:

- spending more money on BPC or undertaking more BPC initiatives
- consistency in both the funding and implementation of these initiatives
- matching BPC efforts with PN objectives and absorptive capacity
- including a sustainment component in the initiatives
- the PN investing its own funds to support or sustain capacity
- the PN having sufficient absorptive capacity
- the PN having high governance indicators
- the PN having a strong economy
- the PN sharing security interests with the United States.

We revisited these results using the four deep-dive case studies to see how the general findings held up in specific cases of BPC in challenging contexts. Of the nine factors identified as strong correlates with success, eight were fully validated in the four

---

[1] Paul, Clarke, et al., 2013.

cases studies, with multiple instances across the cases highlighting the importance of these areas or showing disrupters and difficulties arising when one of these factors was deficient. However, one of the nine previous correlates was *not* validated in these case studies. That was the first one, "spending more money on BPC or undertaking more BPC initiatives." All the cases of BPC in challenging contexts faced practical limits beyond which additional funding or activity was just wasted excess. These limits stemmed from many (and sometimes multiple) sources: limited numbers of personnel or units that had cleared human rights vetting and could be worked with, limited numbers of personnel or units that were willing and able to work with the United States, the limited literacy and baseline competence of PN forces, limited PN bandwidth due to limited numbers of competent and interested PN counterparts in the PN ministry of defense and military services, limitations imposed by the capacity of the ministry to support BPC, and general limitations on the absorptive capacity (in terms of both volume and level) of PN forces in general. Whatever the source, however, the limitations capped the amount of BPC money that could be *effectively* spent in these cases. More money was often spent but was lost or wasted by exceeding the constraints inherent in these challenging contexts.

While the deep-dive case studies emphatically endorsed the other eight correlates of BPC success, two merit further specific mention: the importance of consistency and the importance of sustainment.

Consistency Is Key: Not Just Consistent Funding, but Consistent Objectives, Consistent Agreements, and Consistent Relationships

Previous research has highlighted the importance of consistency in funding and delivery of BPC.[2] The cases examined in this study not only endorse this call for consistency but expand on it. The narratives of these cases highlight numerous instances in which inconsistency damaged BPC efforts. These included not only delays in funding and unnecessary changes to already effective delivery in progress but also changing or conflicting goals or mission scope; changes in levels at which the PN was being engaged (abandoning effectively engaged counterparts); and, perhaps most grievous in the eyes of PN officials, reneging on agreements.[3] In contrast, the case studies revealed progress and success when consistency was maintained. Consistent relationships and training with a specific unit and its officers resulted in notable increases in capacity over time; long-term relationships, even if the U.S. counterpart changed, led to increased mutual respect, more-effective engagement, and greater support for BPC on the PN side.

---

[2]   Paul, Clarke, et al., 2013.

[3]   This is a strong statement, and we wish to emphasize that it is from the perspective of the PN. Of course, the United States did not renege on any formal treaty agreements or agreements at the highest level, but lower-level agreements, plans, or understandings were frequently broken because of administrative changes in programs and efforts, changes in funding and budgetary plans, personnel rotations (deals made with the previous position holder not kept), or changes in human rights–based restrictions.

Without Attention to Sustainment and Maintenance, Capacity Atrophies

Previous research also highlighted the importance of sustainment to BPC success, and these case studies demonstrate that connection. Without attention to the sustainment of capabilities (including refresher training for troops and maintenance of facilities and equipment), they quickly begin to degrade. Troops lose proficiency; units lose proficiency more rapidly as individuals transfer to different units or leave the military (routine personnel processes). Without institutionalizing training (or a robust and ongoing train-the-trainer program), such atrophy is unavoidable. Attention paid to ministerial-level reform and capacity building is time and money well spent in terms of understanding the PN's ability to fund and otherwise support any capacity built after U.S. assistance is no longer available.

The cases revealed even worse levels of decay on the maintenance side. Most of the studied militaries lacked any kind of culture of or training for maintenance. Even when PN forces were willing to do maintenance, lack of training, tools, and parts specific to the equipment the BPC efforts provided doomed that equipment. Road vehicles were used until they stopped, then abandoned by the roadside. Numbers of aircraft or boats slowly decreased as some failed and were then cannibalized in the hope of repairing remaining craft. Short-term successes turned into long-term failure as developed or improved capabilities trended back toward the baseline.[4]

Additional Comparative Observations

In addition to confirming most of the core correlates for BPC success identified in previous research, these case studies provided several important insights. Each is discussed under its own heading in what follows.

Many Challenges Stem from Shortcomings in U.S. Policy or Practice

The significance of lacking consistency and sustainment highlighted in the previous section can be tied to the way in which the United States organizes for and conducts BPC.

DoD organizations typically draw on multiple authorities in a "patchwork" fashion to design the types of activities necessary to do BPC. These authorities come from a wide variety of sources, and the challenge for the BPC planner is to find them and use them appropriately to achieve BPC objectives. In another report,[5] which focused on

---

[4] One reviewer observed (and we agree) that an alternative to planning for sustainment is providing disposable equipment, which is probably well suited to the maintenance cultures of some PNs. A disposable equipment approach, however, would include the same challenge—that built capability would atrophy as equipment failed and needed to be replaced. Under a disposable equipment model, however, this should be less of a surprise.

[5] Jennifer D. P. Moroney, David E. Thaler, and Joe Hogler, *Review of Security Cooperation Mechanisms Combatant Commands Utilize to Build Partner Capacity*, Santa Monica, Calif.: RAND Corporation, RR-413-OSD, 2013.

the CCMDs, we found that the existing patchwork of resources, programs, authorities, processes, and organizational relationships seems to work by and large but is incredibly inefficient at times. We found similar results in our four case studies. The challenges to planning, resourcing, executing, and assessing BPC activities are considerable. Briefly, four factors exemplify some of these challenges. First, statutory authorities for BPC, and security cooperation more widely, vary considerably. Some authorities attached to programs last a single year, and some are multiyear. For example, Section 1206 Global Train and Equip program funds provide one-year funding to fill emergent needs and are not intended to cover sustainment costs, while foreign military financing is granted on an annual basis but provides funding that is longer term and can be used for maintaining existing capabilities. Some limit DoD to engaging only with a PN's military forces, while others allow DoD to engage other security forces, such as those owned by the PN's interior ministry (e.g., paramilitary, police, customs agents, and border guards). Some allow training, while others allow only concept familiarization. Second, resources are unpredictable from year to year and are managed by different agencies working under different priorities. Resources should be obligated as early as possible to secure funding for an event, but that means that events planned later in the calendar year can be at risk of being canceled. In the other extreme, resources left unobligated later in the year can sometimes be used to fund lower-priority activities, merely because the resources are available and need to be obligated quickly. Third, while processes for making it all happen can be streamlined in many cases, they are slow and cumbersome. Planning for exercises, for example, is completed at least a year before the event occurs to ensure that forces are available, etc. Last-minute changes to an event, particularly if another country wants to participate, can mean starting the DoD approval sign-off chain over. Fourth, organizations that have a role in executing BPC activities, even within DoD, play by different rules and priorities. Some coordinate well with the CCMDs, and some not as well.[6] This is not a new or unique finding: Presidential Policy Directive 23, *Security Sector Assistance*, recognizes the need for improved synchronization, planning, and alignment with national security objectives for security sector assistance across the interagency and lays out a number of guidelines for progress in these areas.[7]

Many of the disrupters listed in Chapter Three are partially or completely the fault of the United States. Some are execution and planning failures, but others stem from the way in which the U.S. funds, authorizes, and organizes BPC. The case studies are filled with examples of U.S. processes and procedures producing problems and friction: funding that expires before it can be executed; delays in delivery due to administrative constraints; changes in equipment to be delivered at higher organizational levels, resulting in delivery of suboptimal (or even unusable) equipment; bureaucratic

---

[6]   Moroney, Thaler, and Hogler, 2013.

[7]   White House, Office of the Press Secretary, "Fact Sheet: U.S. Security Sector Assistance Policy," April 5, 2013.

infighting between different departments or organizations; and authorities that stop short of providing training where (and to whom) it would be most beneficial.

Agility Is Lacking

Of particular note in the case studies as a U.S. procedural shortcoming was a lack of agility. In these challenging contexts, the situation on the ground can be very dynamic. Needs change; the attitudes of PN counterparts change; levels and impacts of corruption change. Personnel on the ground (trainers, embassy personnel, and others) were sometimes confronted with situations in which they could have achieved positive progress if they had had authority and options for agility at their level. Several cases included instances that would have benefitted from local control of incentives. For example, in one case we studied, U.S. trainers were unable to threaten to cut off funding when PNs were unwilling to engage in training or to use U.S. equipment as it was intended. Because these flows were controlled at higher levels, PN counterparts were not properly incentivized (sometimes they were rewarded for worsening behavior; sometimes they were punished for improving behavior). Because of a lack of agility, U.S. personnel would sometimes end up delivering BPC to an undermotivated and underperforming unit, even when a much more eager unit was available as an alternative. When needs changed, personnel were sometimes obligated to deliver training that was either less relevant or that had been determined to be too advanced, again because of the lack of agility.

Lack of Partner Willingness Is a Critical Challenge

As will be elaborated in Chapter Three, PN willingness at all levels can contribute to a host of disrupters. The case studies emphasized the importance of partner willingness to the success of any kind for BPC in challenging contexts. When partner stakeholders at all relevant levels were eager to receive, support, and engage in BPC, it was amazing how easily other contextual challenges gave way. Conversely, when partner willingness was low at any relevant stakeholder layer, small hurdles became significant, and simple fixes to small problems became all but impossible. The consensus of the RAND case analysts is that the lack of willingness on the part of the PN is the single most significant challenge among the range of issues that can come up when doing BPC in challenging contexts.

Agreement on Objectives and Approaches Is Key

The case studies also highlighted the importance of agreement on objectives and approaches, both among U.S. stakeholders and between the United States and the PN. Disagreements over objectives or over how to accomplish them can hamstring coordination among U.S. stakeholders and can spoil many factors correlated with success (such as consistency and time lines). Disagreement on objectives or approaches between the United States and the PN can have even worse consequences, the most frequent of which is a general diminution of PN willingness, often with adverse consequences for many aspects of BPC delivery. The cases showed that, when the United States and the PN share an understanding about what the objectives are, a shared time line for their attainment, and an agreed set of approaches and activities to achieve them, many more minor obstacles could be overcome. In contrast, the cases also showed disrupters, disruptions, disagreements, and wasted effort as consequences of misunderstandings about objectives and approaches or of disagreements that endured into execution. For example, in the mid-1990s, the United States sent 73 UH-1 helicopters to Mexico to help with counternarcotics operations. The Mexicans were upset that the equipment was quite dated, apparently from the Vietnam era. As a result, Mexico turned to Russia to purchase MI-8 and MI-17 helicopters, which further complicated U.S.-Mexican relations and negatively affected U.S. efforts to build PN capacity.[8]

Efforts Intentionally and Continuously Fall Just Short of the Termination Condition

Case studies revealed that BPC efforts do not always end after objectives are met. One of the case study interviews revealed the possibility of peculiar specific challenges related to agreement on objectives, one concerning knowing when an objective had been met and what would then happen. Some programs or efforts have clear objectives (a good thing) but are intended to end once the objectives are complete (a good thing from an objective completion point of view but a bad thing for an individual who benefits from the continuation of that effort). The interviewee raised the possibility of collusion between contracted trainers (who would like to continue to be paid to deliver training) and their PN counterparts (who would like to continue to receive U.S. assistance) to have training succeed but not succeed so completely that it is not needed anymore. If the objective was for a 90-percent proficiency rate, after which the program or effort would end, colluding participants aimed for a constant and recurring 89 percent.

This caution is both about objectives articulated in this way and about the incentives for inertia and continuous improvement that never quite reaches the finish line. It is also a caution about who conducts proficiency assessments and whether there are perverse incentives for them to either over- or underestimate changes in proficiency.

Progress in Challenging Contexts Can Be Highly Personality Dependent

Case analysts were surprised at the frequency with which case study narratives revealed that progress or failure had hinged on a single PN counterpart. If such an individual was supportive, they could rally other needed support, effectively work with the PN bureaucracy, fix minor problems, or otherwise grease the wheels. If, on the other hand, such an individual was not supportive, they could drag their feet, delay documents or agreements, mire the bureaucracy, wield their authority to cause delays, or poison the

---

8   John J. Bailey and Roy Godson, *Organized Crime and Democratic Governability: Mexico and the U.S.-Mexican Borderlands*, Pittsburgh, Pa.: University of Pittsburgh Press, 2001.

attitudes of other PN personnel against an effort or program, enabling all manner of additional disrupters.

Depending on the level and power of these personalities, they could be stupendously enabling or horrifically disruptive. In some cases, disruptive individuals were persuaded, cajoled, influenced, or just waited out; dealing with personality-driven barriers required great quantities of patience and finesse and sometimes called for unavailable options for agility (such as the chance to work with a different formation or unit when one unit's commander proved to be extremely unsupportive). In other cases, the benefits of working with an enthusiastic and influential counterpart were not fully appreciated until that individual had moved on to a different assignment, taking the benefits of their efforts with them. For example, in one case country, success was highly personality dependent. A smart, fully engaged chief of a Pacific Command country's coast guard helped consolidate significant gains and set the tone for military professionalism, really enabling significant progress during his tenure.

Ministerial Capacity Proved to Be Extremely Important
All the cases also highlighted the importance of PN ministerial capacity to the effectiveness of BPC. Planning and agreeing to conduct BPC in the initial phases of the progress could be slowed or derailed if PN ministries were not equipped to handle such efforts. Most consequential, however, was the impact of ministries on the postengagement phase. Effective ministerial oversight is required to lay the foundation for avoiding attrition of capabilities. Ministerial involvement is often required to see trained troops used to form units and be deployed as intended. Most critical is the role of the PN ministry in arranging for the sustainment of the capability: refresher and continuing training and plans and funds for maintenance, parts, and replacement equipment. As one case interviewee noted, "The U.S. can spend money forever at the tactical level, but without the ministerial capacity to sustain it, all is for naught—or at the best, will only last as long as the U.S. is willing to sustain it."[9]

More than one case noted limits to the bandwidth of a maturing PN ministry of defense. That is, the fledgling ministry had the capability to do the things needed to support (and arrange for the sustainment of) BPC, but that capability rested with just a few competent leaders and bureaucrats who were capable of doing only so much work before they ran out of hours in the day. Limited ministerial bandwidth of this kind creates a different kind of limit on a PN's absorptive capacity. It may be that a PN is capable of absorbing relatively "deep" capabilities in terms of technical sophistication but that this bandwidth constraint may severely limit the volume of BPC the PN has the capacity to absorb.

---

[9]   Anonymous interview, May 16, 2014.

CHAPTER THREE

Contextual Challenges, Disrupters, and Workarounds

As part of this research, we developed a logic model for BPC training and equipping.[1] The development of this logic model included the identification of possible disrupters, things that can interfere with inputs producing intended outputs, or with outputs resulting in desired outcomes. Many of these disrupters come from the specific cases of BPC in challenging contexts studied as part of this research; others were identified with possible contextual challenges in mind. This chapter presents these disrupters, after some preliminary observations about variations in the ways in which contextual challenges play out and a discussion of appropriate categories.

This listing of possible disrupters should, of itself, be useful to BPC planners. Awareness of things that might go wrong allows contingency planning and preparation of relevant branches and sequels; a problem anticipated is a problem partially solved. (The appendix lists all the disrupters as a concise summary.) Along with the listing and discussion of the disrupters, each section in this chapter also lists possible workarounds. Like the disrupters, many of these workarounds come directly from the empirical cases, although the results of many are mixed. Effective workarounds tend to be highly contextually specific. Still, by listing some of the possible workarounds, we hope to provide some useful suggestions. The discussion includes examples of some of the disrupters and workarounds drawn from historical BPC efforts, although examples were drawn broadly from cases with which we were familiar, not necessarily the cases studied in depth as foundation for this research. This is due to sensitivities associated with the selection of the cases and of some of the details of the cases themselves.

---

[1] The process for developing the logic model is described in Chapter One. A companion report describes the logic model and how it might be used for assessment: Christopher Paul, Brian Gordon, Jennifer D. P. Moroney, Lisa Saum-Manning, Beth Grill, Colin P. Clarke, and Heather Peterson, *A Building Partner Capacity Assessment Framework: Tracking Inputs, Outputs, Outcomes, Disrupters, and Workarounds*, Santa Monica, Calif.: RAND Corporation, RR-935-OSD, 2015. The complete logic model can be downloaded as a spreadsheet from the report page: http://www.rand.org/pubs/research_reports/RR937.html.

Variations in How Contextual Challenges Play Out

During our analyses, we observed that challenges and disrupters can be considered based on variation on a temporal dimension (preengagement, during engagement, postengagement), across different levels (strategic, operational, and tactical), and by origin (U.S. or PN). Preliminary collection of elements for the draft logic model revealed that outputs from one part of the process were inputs to another part of the process. For example, the outputs of the planning process were then inputs to execution. Although this made perfect sense, it provided a challenge for traditional logic modeling, in which inputs and outputs are listed separately. On further examination, we noticed that the sequences of outputs becoming inputs to later processes followed a clear time phase pattern. We experimented with breaking the model into three phases—preengagement, engagement, and postengagement—with each phase having its own set of inputs, activities, outputs, and disrupters. This almost entirely resolved the problem. Under this scheme, outputs of the preengagement phase were often also inputs to the engagement phase but were clearly indicated as outputs in the preengagement portion of the model and as inputs in the engagement portion of the model. We preserved this exploratory separation, and the final model has submodels for each corresponding phase (pre-, during, and post-). Each submodel includes inputs, activities, outputs, disrupters, and workarounds for that phase of the process.

This "pre-, during, post-" division also applied to contextual challenges. When considering what had proven difficult in the cases considered (and why), we noticed variations in when in the process different contextual challenges took effect. We also noted that different challenges or disrupters occurred at different levels. We identified three levels, which roughly correspond to the strategic, operational, and tactical levels (the doctrinal three levels of war).[2] At what we are equating with the strategic level, challenges came from the most senior leadership within the PN or the PN military; were inherent in the PN's economy or national security objectives; or came from U.S. senior leadership, conflicting U.S. national security objectives, or statutory constraints on BPC execution. An example would be a PN's president deciding to terminate visas for all U.S. trainers because of failed negotiations in another aspect of foreign policy. At the equivalent to the operational level, disrupters came from PN military services, the commanders of formations of PN troops or bases, or bases themselves or from U.S. planning processes, difficulties in program management, or challenges stemming from the authorities and approval processes inherent in the patchwork of BPC mechanisms. An example would be a commander deciding not to allow his unit to participate in the training or insisting on different training from what was planned or agreed on. The lowest level, which we equate to the tactical level, included the interactions between PN trainees and U.S. trainers, the details of facilities, or small-scale logistics. Examples

---

2   Joint Publication 3-0, *Joint Operations*, Washington, D.C.: U.S. Department of Defense, August 11, 2011.

would be the level of motivation of the troops in training, their level of preparation for training, or the condition of their uniforms (not as trivial as it might sound at first blush: Inadequate footwear can seriously affect the ability to conduct field exercises). Challenges could play out at multiple levels simultaneously: The level of preparation of training troops creates a tactical concern for trainers but may have been the result of a strategic- or operational-level decision not to send troops that were better prepared to participate.

Further, we noted that similar challenges played out differently in different contexts: For example, corruption within the PN was a challenge common to many cases. However, that could play out at the operational level in the preengagement phase, with funds allocated for facility improvement being squandered or diverted, or tactically during the engagement phase, with trainees selling their allocations of ammunition for a live-fire exercise to buy drugs or food.

Finally, we noted that, while some of the disrupters observed in the cases were indeed contextual challenges, they were brought to the context by the United States rather than by the PN. How the United States is organized and authorized to conduct BPC has certain inherent complexities and weaknesses and certain vulnerabilities in execution. When categorizing challenges and disrupters, the partner source for the challenge is also important to note. Taking these three categories (temporal phase, level, and origin) together creates a useful framework for better understanding disrupters and challenges and, more importantly, identifying opportunities to make improvements.

Input and Disrupter Categories

In addition to the division based on where (at what level) and when (pre-, during, post-) disrupters and challenges play out, other categorizations from the overall logic model are useful here. Because the logic model is divided horizontally by arraying the sequential phases from left to right and arraying inputs to outputs from left to right within phases, there is space for vertical divisions as well. These vertical divisions are categories that put like sequences of action next to each other. Since the primary organizing principle in creating these categories ended up corresponding very closely to grouping like inputs with like, we label these categories *input categories*. The model contains ten input categories:

- U.S. program goals and plans
- U.S. political will
- PN political will
- funding
- PN personnel (trainees)
- U.S. trainers

- equipment (to be trained on)
- logistics and transport
- facilities (including security)
- curriculum, program of instruction (POI), and training content.

Thus, the overall structure of the logic model runs the input categories as rows, and the sequential phases (pre-, during, post-) as columns, with each phase containing corresponding phase inputs, activities, disrupters, workarounds, and outputs (see Figure 3.1).

All the disrupters and workarounds presented in this chapter can be found in the logic model. For presentation here, we identified an organizing principle specific to disrupters. Because a disrupter can affect multiple input areas and because broader contextual challenges play out differently by contributing to specific disrupters in different input areas, we logically grouped disrupters based on the following categories,

Figure 3.1
Notional Organization of the Building Partner Capacity Training and Equipping Logic Model

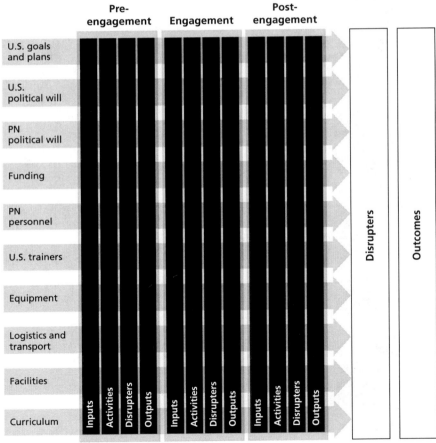

RAND *RR937-3.1*

beginning first with disrupter categories pertaining to or originating in U.S. BPC processes, moving on to relational disrupter categories that involve both the United States and the PN, and concluding with primarily PN-origin disruptions:

- objectives and goals
- U.S. internal contention
- U.S. continuity and agility
- U.S. trainers
- U.S.-PN relationships
- curriculum and training materials
- equipment mismatch
- sustainment
- corruption or governance
- human rights violations and restrictions
- security situation
- PN willingness to support and conduct BPC
- PN willingness to organize for increased capacity
- PN personnel and trainees
- PN infrastructure, facilities, and logistics.

The next section describes each category of disrupters, lists the identified disrupters, and describes some of the possible workarounds.

Disrupters and Workarounds, by Disrupter Category

As noted in Chapter One, logic model elements (including disrupters and workarounds) were collected both inductively and deductively. That means that some disrupters are based on actual experiences in the cases and some are notional and could happen but were not observed in the cases considered here. In fact, the vast majority of disrupters listed here did occur, at least to some extent, in at least one of the four cases. Even when a disrupter was initially generated from a logical exercise, disrupters were tested when the logic model was demonstrated on the empirical cases. In what follows, all disrupters appeared in at least one of the four case studies unless offset in *italics*.

The suggested workarounds were not tested to the same extent. Fewer of the workarounds appeared in the actual cases, and results were often mixed when they did. Listed workarounds are possible solutions but are just a few of a wider range of possible solutions. Those confronting disrupters should certainly consider listed workarounds but should also consider other avenues and solutions because the best approach to resolving some of these issues can vary depending on the personalities involved and the cultural context.

In what follows, we have organized the disrupters and workarounds by the 15 disrupter categories.

A Note About the Relationship Between Disrupters and Inputs

Before the listing of the disrupters, however, a brief discussion of the relationship between disrupters and inputs seems prudent. As noted previously, traditional logic models do not include disrupters. In fact, it is possible to use only the traditional logic model categories (inputs, outputs, and outcomes) and still capture disrupters in the model by specifying the input as being free of the disrupter. For example, if an observed disrupter concerned trainees arriving for training either fatigued or intoxicated and if that was interfering with training, you could, instead of listing that disrupter in a disrupters category, list the input as being "sufficient number of trainees, all of whom are free from fatigue and intoxication." Almost all disrupters could be listed as inputs in this way, and the balance between inputs and disrupters is as much art as science. We have sought to strike a useful balance, with our goal being inputs specified to include what one might optimistically expect and disrupters capturing either what one might pessimistically expect or things that one would *not* reasonably expect (because challenging contexts sometimes produce fairly unreasonable episodes).

We make this note to point out that the list of disrupters is not (and does not appear to be) exhaustive. However, it becomes much more comprehensive if considered alongside all the inputs and with the recognition that the logic of a logic model requires an unbroken chain, all critical inputs producing all critical outputs and outcomes, without any disrupters sufficiently present to disrupt the outputs or outcomes.

Disrupter Category: Objectives and Goals

As our previous work on assessment and the received wisdom in the area asserts, effective assessment requires clear, realistic, and measurable goals.[3] For assessment, objectives should be specific, measurable, attainable, results oriented, and time bound (SMART). This advice extends beyond assessment to goal accomplishment. Certainly, it is a struggle to measure the accomplishment of objectives if they are not clear, but it is also hard to achieve goals if they are not clear. Disrupters in this category relate to changing goals, impractical goals, or disconnects between goals and practices. These specific disrupters (listed in Table 3.1) capture ways in which problems with defining or establishing goals have (or might have) interfered with the logic of BPC between inputs and outputs (or outputs and outcomes) in the empirical cases. Table 3.1 also lists the

---

[3] See, for example, Christopher Paul, Jessica M. Yeats, Colin P. Clarke, and Miriam Mathews, *Assessing and Evaluating Efforts to Inform, Influence, and Persuade: Desk Reference*, Santa Monica, Calif.: RAND Corporation, RR-809/1-OSD, 2015; Michael J. McNerney, Jennifer D. P. Moroney, Peter Mandaville, and Terry Hagen, *New Security and Justice Sector Partnership Models: Implications of the Arab Uprisings*, Santa Monica, Calif.: RAND Corporation, RR-605-DOS, 2014.

Table 3.1
Disrupters: Objectives and Goals

Disrupter	Input Category
U.S. goals are unrealistic in terms of capability improvement or time required	U.S. program goals
Attainment of standards is not likely in the time and resources allotted	Curriculum, POI, training content
Standards are not matched to baseline proficiency of PN trainees	Curriculum, POI, training content
Objectives or mission scope changes	U.S. political will
Projected U.S. funds are insufficient, and funding is used up prior to completion of program	Funding
Medical personnel are not aware of training demands and disqualify trainees unnecessarily or clear them inappropriately	Logistics and transport

NOTE: In this and subsequent tables, all disrupters appeared in at least one of the four case studies unless offset in italics.

input categories under which these disrupters can be found in the full BPC training and equipping logic model.

Possible workarounds for disrupters in objectives and goals depend on the specifics of the issue with the goals or objectives. If the goal is sound but is not understood (or not being faithfully pursued) at a subordinate level, additional engagement, explanation, or monitoring and supervision may be sufficient. However, if goals are flawed (not meeting one or more of the SMART criteria), they may need to be revisited and revised. The following are some of the specific possible workarounds included in the logic model:

- Break plan into increments by fiscal year and establish review procedures to ensure standards are being met and training is appropriate.
- Engage PN counterparts to alter the training time line or revisit standards.
- Have the embassy and/or CCMD monitor the training program.

Disrupter Category: U.S. Internal Contention

Internal contention between U.S. stakeholders is a significant category of potential disrupters. Disagreements can be between departments (between the departments of Defense and State or among the departments of the Treasury, Homeland Security, Justice, and State), between organizations (the Defense Security Cooperation Agency and the Office of the Under Secretary of Defense for Policy), between commands and components, between the embassy and executing personnel, or within any of these elements. Such contention can involve both the debate, discussion, and disagreement itself and the resistance to an effort once a decision has been made (either as a compromise that one party is not pleased with or as one element exercising its authority to limit disagreement). Decisions about the type of aircraft and training the United States was to provide for Iraq (in response to Iraq's request for advanced F-16 jets and, more recently, Apache combat helicopters), for example, was the subject of significant debate in Congress and within the security cooperation bureaucracy.[4] Table 3.2 lists specific disrupters from the logic model for this category.

Workarounds focus first on reaching agreement. If there is a disagreement on facts, it is necessary to work harder to establish the facts. A preengagement needs assessment of partner capabilities can provide a good planning point and a good source of data from which to build consensus. When personalities conflict or organizational interests do not perfectly coincide, discussions at the lowest possible level may help identify genuine differences and possible effective compromises, which can then be elevated for approval. If a solution cannot be found through low-level engagement, escalation to the next level within respective organizations may help find common ground. Encouraging debate early but setting deadlines for key decisions is another way to seek consensus. If a key stakeholder is just not engaged, find ways to encourage engagement, such as visits from senior stakeholders from other organizations, invitations to view training activities, or invitations to participate in other ways. Other workarounds might help reduce the opportunities for disagreements, such as the development of a stronger interagency-supported prioritization process for BPC.

Disrupter Category: U.S. Continuity and Agility

BPC efforts can struggle mightily over time when there are breaks in continuity (particularly of funding, year to year) or when conditions change but efforts do not change

Table 3.2
Disrupters: Internal Contention

Disrupter	Input Category
There is disagreement on PN needs for training	U.S. program goals
There is disagreement on resourcing	U.S. program goals
There is disagreement on methodology	U.S. program goals
There is disagreement on program longevity	U.S. program goals
There is disagreement over who pays	U.S. program goals
Stakeholders continue to argue for modifications to the BPC plan	U.S. program goals
There is resistance at congressional, OSD, and CCMD levels	U.S. political will
There is resistance from the in-country team (embassy or military group)	U.S. political will
Embassy officials are focused on other efforts and are not involved once training begins	U.S. political will

---

4   "Senate Moves Toward Supporting U.S. Helicopters for Iraq," Reuters, January 9, 2014.

to keep pace with them. This disrupter category captures breaks in continuity or lacking agility on the U.S. side. For example, one downside of the Section 1206 Global Train and Equip program is that it provides only one- or two-year funding support. As a result, PNs may develop new counterterrorism capabilities that can then be sustained only through other funding mechanisms or their own country's limited resources.[5] Table 3.3 lists specific disrupters.

Workarounds depend on the specific form of break in continuity or lack of agility that threatens. Workarounds are sparse for some aspects of the problem, with legislative changes or changes in authorities necessary to allow multiyear funding or increased flexibility.[6] Specific possible workarounds identified in the logic model include the following:

- Assign only U.S. personnel who will be available throughout the program or for a required amount of time.
- Engage an appropriate attaché or other U.S. official who can work with the PN over the long term.
- Delay the beginning of the program or resource it from other sources.
- Appropriate funds so that the in-country team has maximum opportunity for agility.
- Appropriate funds with two- or three-year money, if possible.

Table 3.3
Disrupters: Continuity and Agility

Disrupter	Input Category
There is no continuity (personnel rotations, etc.)	U.S. program goals
Momentum is lost after original training event	U.S. political will
There are delays in funding or obligation of funds	Funding
In-country team cannot redirect funds when problems arise	Funding
Funds do not carry into following years	Funding
Resources are reallocated at a higher level during program	Funding
Military construction funds are not available or not permitted for training	Facilities (including security)

---

[5] Jennifer D. P. Moroney, Beth Grill, Joe Hogler, Lianne Kennedy Boudali, and Christopher Paul, *How Successful Are U.S. Efforts to Build Capacity in Developing Countries? A Framework to Assess the Global Train and Equip "1206" Program*, Santa Monica, Calif.: RAND Corporation, TR-1121-OSD, 2011.

[6] Although short-term workarounds are lacking, recognition of the challenge may be useful input to future congressional committee work on changes to existing authorities or the development of new programs.

Disrupter Category: Trainers

There are a number of ways that lack of preparation for trainers or inadequate execution by trainers can prevent training from being effective. Table 3.4 displays trainer-related disrupters identified in the logic model.

Workarounds focus on better preparation (or selection) of and support for trainers. Possible workarounds identified in the logic model include the following:

- Contract interpreters with necessary technical expertise.
- Select trainers with previous experience in country or in countries with similar cultures.
- Conduct cultural familiarization training for U.S. personnel prior to deployment.
- Conduct a predeployment orientation session for trainers to cover the training plan and expectations.
- Review contracted translator performance, trainer qualifications, or cultural training for effectiveness.
- Implement course monitoring by U.S. program personnel and embassy team.
- Pair trainers with PN cadres who will be present in classes, share office space, etc.
- Arrange for a third party (allied nation, regional partner, contractor with experience) to participate or take the lead in training.

Disrupter Category: U.S.-PN Relationships

One of the most difficult aspects of BPC in challenging contexts can be U.S.-PN relationships at all levels. Challenges can emerge from the highest level, in the geopolitical bilateral or multilateral relationships between the United States and the PN, on down to the lowest levels, the interactions between U.S. trainers and PN trainees, and at every level in between. Political disagreements between heads of state on threat priorities can be major stumbling blocks for BPC, in which a PN leader may prefer to prioritize combating a local insurgent group, while the United States would prefer to make more-global extremist organizations the top priority. At a lower level, military

Table 3.4
Disrupters: Trainers

Disrupter	Input Category
Trainers are insufficiently familiar with PN languages and customs	U.S. trainers
Trainers are unfamiliar with goals and intent of the training	U.S. trainers
Trainers are not communicating with PN personnel effectively	U.S. trainers
Trainers deviate from plan	U.S. trainers
PN trainees do not respect the trainers because of rank or civilian status	U.S. trainers
PN officials, commanders, or students do not find U.S. trainers credible or trustworthy	U.S. trainers

commanders may be unwilling to engage with U.S. trainers because of anti-Western views or because the commanders perceive U.S. engagement as a direct threat to their own power or influence. Specific disrupters address myriad aspects of the relationships, from individual person-to-person connections, to broader cultural misunderstandings, to the number of personnel assigned to certain interactions, to mismatches in rank or authority across a liaison, to specific points of disagreement. Table 3.5 lists the disrupters from the logic model belonging to this category.

Workarounds depend on the level of the relationship problem and the context. Misunderstandings can often be resolved through engagement and repetition. Patience may seem to slow the overall process but can actually be essential to some relationships and can facilitate progress. For example, we received an anecdote regarding one country case in which problems with the corrupt sale of high-quality aviation fuel and its replacement with lower-quality fuel were (eventually) resolved through patience and careful and diplomatic engagement with the commander of the relevant PN formation. In some cases, appealing to personal relationships may work, but in others, such

Table 3.5
Disrupters: U.S.-PN Relationships

Disrupter	Input Category
U.S. personnel lack understanding of PN structures and personnel	U.S. program goals
U.S. or PN facilitators deviate from agreed-to plans	U.S. program goals
Insufficient or excess U.S. personnel are assigned to cover PN interactions	U.S. program goals
U.S. is unable to reach or engage senior PN officials	U.S. program goals
U.S. approach to PN officials is coordinated poorly; officials are approached out of sequence or not by the correct U.S. stakeholder	U.S. program goals
PN officials are too quick to believe U.S. involvement is no longer required	PN political will
There is disagreement between what PN wants and what the United States thinks the PN needs	PN political will
PN leaders receive inflated view of new capability and increase risk-prone behavior	PN political will
PN counterparts change	PN political will
Culture clashes occur within PN forces	PN personnel (trainees)
U.S. and PN disagree on the role of equipment in the training program	Equipment (to be trained on)
PN does not believe the equipment is necessary or appropriate to do the training	Equipment (to be trained on)
U.S. and PN disagree over measures of student competence	PN political will
U.S. and PN disagree on the utility of the instructional materials	Curriculum, POI, training content

appeals may be seen as inappropriate shortcuts outside the chain of command. Specific possible workarounds identified in logic model development include the following:

- Engage PN officials within the United States (or at the United Nations) to determine receptiveness to BPC and get recommendations for appropriate counterparts.
- Supervise training with U.S. and PN representatives from the in-country team and ministry.
- Engage PN counterparts to adjust the number of U.S. personnel during the program, if required.
- Brief senior U.S. policymakers on the program and their interactions with PN counterparts.
- Designate the embassy team as the message coordinator.
- Ensure enriched and continued engagement with PN officials.
- Focus training on civil-military culture-specific issues.
- Suspend the activity and reengage appropriate decisionmakers.
- Establish standards and testing guidelines jointly with PN officials.

Disrupter Category: Curriculum and Training Materials

Flaws in or problems with the curriculum, POI, or training or instructional materials can also become disrupters. Table 3.6 lists disrupters in this category.

Identified possible workarounds are simple and straightforward: Modify, revise, or update training plans or materials as needed. When appropriate, include PN counterparts in curriculum development or revision.

Table 3.6
Disrupters: Curriculum and Training Materials

Disrupter	Input Category
Training is insufficient to permit intended operations or to achieve standards	PN personnel (trainees) and curriculum, POI, training content
Equipment is not part of the training curriculum	Equipment (to be trained on)
Manuals were not written in the correct language or at a level that PN personnel can understand	Equipment (to be trained on)
Manuals were not cleared through foreign disclosure or copyright process	Equipment (to be trained on)
Curriculum does not follow a form familiar to trainees	Curriculum, POI, training content
Curriculum becomes outdated quickly	Curriculum, POI, training content

Disrupter Category: Equipment Mismatch

This disrupter category covers a range of situations that adversely affect BPC because the PN does not have needed materiel, either because needed equipment was not provided or because the equipment provided was not the right equipment. It is often difficult to know what equipment PN forces already have (as well as its state of repair and their proficiency with it), and the equipment provided may not be a good match for a number of reasons (mistaken assumptions about PN troop skills and qualifications, partner force inability to maintain equipment, miscommunication about required equipment, or required equipment not available as excess defense articles). Examples abound of PNs receiving advanced military equipment through the Excess Defense Articles program that is inappropriate for the PN's purposes or that the PN is unable to sustain. Table 3.7 summarizes the equipment mismatch–related disrupters from the logic model.

Workarounds are fairly intuitive (a problem well-articulated is a problem half solved) and correspond to one of two general approaches. First, work with what is available. Scope training to correspond to available equipment and proficiency, adjust the training to include available materials, or delay certain aspects of curriculum until additional equipment or increased familiarity becomes available. Second, find ways to get needed equipment. Contract with a third party to provide needed parts or ammunition. Revisit the procurement process, working harder to get the right equipment to the partner.

Table 3.7
Disrupters: Equipment Mismatch

Disrupter	Input Category
PN is limited by the types or age of its existing equipment	PN political will and equipment (to be trained on)
The equipment procured is insufficient or differs from what the in-country team requested	Equipment (to be trained on)
PN cannot provide ammunition and requires a type not in U.S. inventory	Equipment (to be trained on)
PN cannot provide parts and requires parts not in the U.S. inventory	Equipment (to be trained on)
PN personnel are not sufficiently familiar with the equipment to conduct safe exercises	Equipment (to be trained on)
PN lacks absorptive capacity to utilize information technology systems beyond training periods	Facilities (including security)

Disrupter Category: Sustainment

One of the main findings from one of our previous reports is the importance of sustainment efforts to the success of BPC (an observation confirmed in this research).[7] By sustainment, we mean efforts to maintain and continue the effectiveness of built capabilities, including the maintenance of equipment and facilities, and the preservation (and institutionalization) of a training pipeline, refresher training for trained forces, and other efforts (such as maintenance contracts) to see that capacity built endures beyond the next rotation of the initial individual recipients. The biggest disrupter of all in this category would be to totally ignore sustainment considerations. In one case, a lack of any kind of sustainment planning left a PN's coast guard with just one working patrol boat. As a defense official described to us, the PN suffered because it was given many brand-new boats but no tools or spares (and clearly lacked the resources to develop an indigenous maintenance capacity). Failure to plan for sustainment does not appear explicitly in the disrupter listing because several sustainment considerations are listed as inputs in the logic model, so their absence is an input failure rather than a disrupter between inputs and outputs. This disrupter category captures many of the things that can work against effective maintenance, with many broader sustainment considerations left as part of inputs. Table 3.8 lists the identified disrupters.

Table 3.8
Disrupters: Sustainment

Disrupter	Input Category
U.S. disagreements exist on sustainment funding	U.S. program goals and plans
PN does not agree to focus on sustainment and maintenance	PN political will
PN officials are content to permit continued U.S. handling of functions that the PN could perform	PN political will
PN does not allocate resources to continue training	PN political will
Maintenance and training standards are not adhered to	PN personnel (trainees)
Third-party trainers are not able to commit to involvement in future iterations	U.S. trainers
PN personnel are unaccustomed to performing or unwilling to perform daily maintenance actions	Equipment (to be trained on)
PN lacks appropriate personnel on hand for maintenance	Equipment (to be trained on)
PN does not keep up preventive maintenance practices	Equipment (to be trained on)
U.S. applies a contractor support model that the PN cannot carry forward	Facilities

---

[7] Paul, Clarke, et al., 2013.

The possible workarounds we identified correspond closely with specific disrupters:

- Notify the PN that U.S. effort will not be expended without a viable sustainment plan following the program.
- Outline "scaling back" of U.S. involvement with each interaction of training.
- Focus on training the trainer and quickly build an indigenous training capacity.
- Build an institutionalized training cadre that can become self-sustaining.
- Include maintenance training as a requirement of training completion.
- Examine and, if necessary, assist with ministerial-level reform to ensure that tactical- and operational-level capabilities receive high-level support for sustainment purposes.
- Consider all equipment to be disposable and plan for periodic wholesale replacement, rather than any kind of maintenance.
- Build a sustainment plan based on PN capabilities, not defaulting to the U.S. way of doing things.

Disrupter Category: Corruption or Governance

A common contextual challenge is poor PN governance and endemic corruption. These disrupters are all ways in which these two challenges can, individually or jointly, play out in (and interfere with) BPC efforts. Table 3.9 lists corruption- and governance-related disrupters from the logic model.

Workarounds for corruption or poor governance follow one of several forms. The first is to work through it, accepting certain delays and losses, adding more inputs (knowing some will be lost to corruption), expanding time lines, focusing on shared objectives with PN counterparts, and noting how corruption is preventing attainment of the shared objectives. The second is to promote reform or enforcement on the part of the PN. Such reform is often the ideal path but may be time consuming or may just not be something the PN is ready and willing to do. The third is to limit the opportunities for corruption or poor governance to have an effect by keeping funds and equipment under U.S. control for as much of the process as possible, warehousing equipment in country under U.S. control, disbursing equipment or ammunition immediately before its use, returning training equipment to U.S. control at the completion of training, etc. The final form of workaround is to withdraw U.S. support. Withdrawal of support is not really a "workaround" because it cannot lead to BPC success in the short term and does not contribute positively in the short term to whatever U.S. national security objectives the BPC was intended to support. However, withdrawal of support does prevent waste, removes perverse incentives (rewards to the corrupt), and may increase U.S. credibility or otherwise set the stage for more-effective pursuit of national security objectives at a later time.

Table 3.9
Disrupters: Corruption or Governance

Disrupter	Input Category
Corruption diverts funding or other resources	Funding
Pay is unequal compared with other PN military services	PN personnel (trainees)
PN does not release or diverts equipment prior to training	Equipment (to be trained on)
Ammunition is diverted from training, or PN personnel sell ammunition	Equipment (to be trained on)
Equipment is diverted posttraining	Equipment (to be trained on)
PN does not establish part-release procedures or loses parts to corruption	Equipment (to be trained on)
Disbursing funds is difficult in country	Funding
Delivery of material is delayed or impeded by customs or bureaucracy	Logistics and transport
PN corruption leads to poor fuel quality	Logistics and transport
PN laws do not support the U.S. training mission and the status of U.S. trainers sufficiently	Logistics and transport
PN funds are exhausted or halted due to instability or other reasons beyond counterparts' control	Funding

Disrupter Category: Human Rights Violations and Restrictions

A subcategory of U.S.-PN relationships concerns human rights. Aspects of this category also fundamentally concern goals and objectives because the tension between encouraging human rights and conducting BPC comes from trying to pursue two different objectives simultaneously. Simply put, efforts to encourage good human rights behavior (or avoid positive reinforcement to those who have not respected human rights in the past) often interfere with BPC efforts. This is all right; when the U.S. Congress prioritizes human rights, some aspects of the relationship with the PN (including BPC) may become difficult or strained. Within the context of our framework, this kind of suspension, disruption, or additional vetting burden is a disrupter in the sense that it makes BPC more difficult and success less likely, but these things may also be good in their own right and important contributors to broader U.S. foreign policy goals. Similarly, if we talk about workarounds to the constraints that human rights–promoting sanctions or processes impose, we are *not* discussing ways to suborn congressional intent but are simply using the same language we use throughout to discuss how effective BPC might continue while respecting the restrictions and constraints and encouraging better behavior.

Human rights–based constraints primarily take one of two forms: either a suspension of funding or activity or a restriction on engagement (to certain areas, to certain units or services, or to individuals who have been appropriately vetted). Military coups or other forms of unacceptable behavior can lead to similar interruptions. Disrupters related to suspensions of engagement are captured primarily as inputs because such suspensions preclude generation of many needed inputs (funding, authorities, etc.). Specific disrupters related to vetting and engagement restrictions that were identified in the logic model are listed in Table 3.10.

Workarounds are, again, not intended to try to circumvent the human rights restrictions but to find ways to accomplish the BPC mission while still respecting the restrictions. Possibilities include the following:

- Identify larger numbers of candidate trainees from acceptable entities and organizations.
- Change the training locations or the types of training provided.
- Maintain a U.S. presence to monitor PN operations or consider suspending assistance.
- Delay beginning of the program until funding can be opened to all necessary activities.
- Train personnel immediately after basic training.
- Request that the PN establish a new unit that is not engaged in disqualifying activities.
- Engage the U.S. in-country team early to complete screening.
- Identify additional sources of funding not tied to congressional restrictions (but still subject to internationally accepted human rights vetting standards).
- Leverage other regional players that are actively conducting BPC activities in the PN.

Working in contexts in which human rights are a concern can take extra time and require extra attention. In the early 1990s, for example, following the Chapultepec

Table 3.10
Disrupters: Human Rights Violations and Restrictions

Disrupter	Input Category
Activities are restricted to certain activities or interactions with specific PN entities	U.S. political will and funding
Accusations are made about additional human rights or abuses	U.S. political will
Insufficient personnel who have cleared the vetting process are available	PN personnel (trainees)
Bureaucratic hurdles to vetting exist	PN personnel (trainees)

Accords, U.S. security assistance helped improve the accountability and human rights practices of the Salvadoran police. It would take some time for the human rights training to take root. Yet this was an essential first step to developing an internal security force with legitimacy *and* the ability to combat El Salvador's suite of threats, from gang violence to drug trafficking.[8]

Disrupter Category: Security Situation

The final disrupter category concerns disrupters that come directly from the security situation. These include the level of permissiveness of the environment and constraints imposed by force protection (FP) requirements. For example, in 2011, both the United States and the United Kingdom withdrew trainers working with Pakistan's frontier constabulary when the security situation in their area of operations deteriorated.[9] Higher levels of FP were mandated after the attack on the U.S. embassy in Benghazi in 2012. Table 3.11 lists the disrupters in this category.

Workarounds cannot really attack the underlying problem (the level of security threat or insecurity in the country) but instead focus on meeting, or lightening, FP requirements. Possible workarounds listed in the logic model include the following:

- Coordinate with in-country team for appropriate FP plans.
- Engage U.S. special operations forces (SOF) to conduct training (SOF have fewer FP requirements).
- Reconsider the training location (to include the possibility of using a third country).

Table 3.11
Disrupters: Security Situation

Disrupter	Input Category
It is difficult to move U.S. trainers safely to the training facility	Logistics and transport
Extracting U.S. trainers in the event of natural disaster, security breach, etc., is challenging	Logistics and transport
Training conditions necessitate housing U.S. personnel at separate location	Facilities (including security)
FP requirements cannot be met	Facilities (including security)
PN modifies facilities after U.S. departure so that they are no longer FP compliant	Facilities (including security)

---

[8] Seth G. Jones, Olga Oliker, Peter Chalk, C. Christine Fair, Rollie Lal, and James Dobbins, *Securing Tyrants or Fostering Reform? U.S. Internal Security Assistance to Repressive and Transitioning Regimes*, Santa Monica, Calif.: RAND Corporation, MG-550-OSI, 2006, p. 24.

[9] "UK Military Trainers in Pakistan Are Withdrawn," BBC, June 27, 2011.

- Inform PN counterparts that future U.S. involvement will depend on meeting FP requirements.

Disrupter Category: PN Willingness to Support or Conduct BPC

One of the most common disrupters encountered in the cases of BPC in the contexts we studied was a lack of willingness on the part of PN representatives at any and all levels. Motives varied: lack of interest, competing priorities (both in terms of interest in doing BPC and in terms of allocation of individuals' time and attention), inability to perceive benefit (to the country, the service, or themselves), political considerations, fear of risk, and others. In one case, a military commander simply refused to allow U.S. trainers on base. In another case, the PN allowed the local press to identify the intended-to-be-secure location where U.S. trainers were residing, which severely compromised their safety.

The consequences, however, varied less: important things not getting done, not getting done on time, or not getting done adequately and thereby interfering with progression along the logic of BPC. Table 3.12 lists disrupters identified in the logic model that connect to lack of willingness to begin or complete planned BPC activities.

Workarounds for deficient willingness are difficult and highly contextually specific, often coming down to matters of personality or individual proclivities. Willingness can often be a show-stopper; in our BPC training and equipping logic model, the most frequently listed workaround for disrupters in this category is "suspend activity and reengage appropriate decisionmakers."[10] This workaround amounts to stopping the activity until you can find someone who is willing to support, allow, or participate. Another category of common workarounds suggests doing whatever it is that needs to be done with U.S. funding, personnel, or assets. In one case in the Central Command AOR, U.S. trainers responded to a PN unit's repeated unwillingness to engage by shifting their efforts to focus on a different PN unit that was operating nearby. This creative workaround not only resulted in more-effective training but also had the added benefit of making the initial (bypassed) unit interested in reengaging with the United States later and on much better terms. Other possible workarounds involve using PN leadership or senior personnel to visit, observe, participate, or otherwise encourage the willingness of their subordinates (but is of course contingent on the willingness of the leaders themselves).

Disrupter Category: PN Willingness to Organize for Increased Capacity

This disrupter category is fundamentally similar to the previous one, and concerns PN reluctance or refusal to do things necessary for the success of the BPC process. Here, disrupters focus specifically on lack of willingness after the BPC training or equipment delivery, on the things that must be done to realize actual improvements in

---

[10] Paul, Gordon, et al., 2015.

Table 3.12
Disrupters: PN Willingness to Support or Conduct BPC

Disrupter	Input Category
PN government and ministerial-level support are not communicated to or not shared by frontline units and personnel	PN political will
PN support is lacking because of honest misunderstanding or translation issues	PN political will
PN officials are focused on other efforts and are not involved once training begins	PN political will
PN is afraid U.S. assistance will unbalance internal power dynamic and so is resistant	PN political will
PN does not fund transfer of personnel	PN personnel (trainees)
PN slow-rolls the process or assigns inferior personnel to the program	PN personnel (trainees)
PN trainees are not assigned in a timely manner	PN personnel (trainees)
PN is reluctant to "waste" equipment operations on training	Equipment (to be trained on)
Transport resources are used for other purposes or missions	Logistics and transport
Authorities are not established for release of parts and fuel	Logistics and transport
PN is reluctant to provide access to examine facilities	Facilities (including security)
PN officials are reluctant to have U.S. personnel living near the training facility	Facilities (including security)
PN will not permit changes or procedures that would conform with FP requirements	Facilities (including security)
PN is unwilling or unable to provide facility staff	Facilities (including security)

capacity once training and equipment have been delivered. Sometimes PN willingness relates to disconnects between U.S. objectives and PN objectives. For example, in the 1990s, the United States provided substantial counternarcotics support to Colombia. To Washington's consternation, Bogota often tasked troops trained with resources for counternarcotics for other purposes, such as counterterrorism or counterinsurgency. In 2002, President George W. Bush signed National Security Policy Directive 18, "Supporting Policy in Columbia." This directive expanded the authority of DoD and the Department of State to work with the Colombian military in waging a counterinsurgency campaign against FARC. One of the main pillars of this campaign would be U.S. efforts to work with Joint Task Force Omega. The task force's strategy was to fight against FARC, as well as to offensively attack drug trafficking organizations and para-militaries. Since the insurgents sustained their campaign of violence through funds acquired through the drug trade, going after both the narcotics and the insurgents was within the Colombian military's rules of engagement. Table 3.13 lists the disrupters in this category.[11]

Workarounds are similar to those listed for the previous willingness category, with the logic model offering a few additional specific possibilities:

- Include sustainment and program improvement measures in the coordinated plan.
- Plan dual-purpose BPC activities that satisfy both governments.
- Maintain a U.S. presence to monitor PN operations and consider suspension of assistance, renegotiation of the program, or shifting of effort to other units.

The building of dual-use humanitarian assistance and disaster recovery capabilities is a perfect example of this type of workaround. For example, high-speed, ocean-

Table 3.13
Disrupters: PN Willingness to Organize for Increased Capacity

Disrupter	Input Category
PN shows no interest or ability in sustaining program results	U.S. program goals
PN supports BPC efforts but does not prioritize the mission that BPC is intended to enhance	PN political will
There is no indication that PN officials plan to change operations or use trainees as intended (or according to U.S. objectives)	PN political will
Trained personnel not used as intended (not assigned to take advantage of training received)	PN personnel (trainees)
PN creates temporary composite units to receive training and equipment (and spread resources across PN stakeholders), then disbands the units	PN personnel (trainees)
PN personnel are not allowed to use new equipment after completion of training	Equipment (to be trained on)
PN personnel do not choose to use new equipment after completion of training	Equipment (to be trained on)
PN policy does not permit deployment for international operations	Curriculum, POI, training content

---

[11] For the challenges of balancing Colombia's counternarcotics and counterinsurgency campaigns simultaneously, see Felbab-Brown, 2009, pp. 69–112. For more on National Security Presidential Directive 18, see James J. Mathis, "Solving Colombia's Problems," Carlisle, Pa.: U.S. Army War College, 2003, p. 14. For more on Joint Task Force Omega, see David E. Spencer, Carlos O. Ospina, David R. Moreno, Alejandro Arbelaez, Juan Carlos Gomez, Carlos Berrios, and Jorge L. Vargas, "Colombia's Road to Recovery: Security and Governance 1982–2010," National Defense University, Center for Hemispheric Defense Studies, 2011.

going vessels (35–40 ft) and smaller, shallow-draft skiffs (20–30 ft) can be used to respond to humanitarian assistance and disaster recovery imperatives and for riverine and mangrove area patrols to clear out ungoverned spaces and take away terrorists' sanctuary.

Disrupter Category: PN Personnel and Trainees

This disrupter category comprises the host of things that can go wrong with PN trainees, from problems with their assignment to training activities and the ability to arrive at them to deficiencies in baseline preparation. Having the right number of adequately prepared trainees available to participate in the full duration of the training program is easy to take for granted as an input, but examination of the cases has revealed numerous things that can prevent this foundational building block to BPC success from being laid. In the cases we studied, trainee attention and attendance were curtailed for a surprisingly wide range of reasons. For example, in one case, a high operational tempo (OPTEMPO) prevented a sufficient number of trainees from being available. In another case, trainees were discouraged by their commanders from engaging with U.S. trainers for political reasons. In other cases, some trainees were simply unmotivated due to low pay and a lack of incentive for training or simply too drunk or high to show up at the appropriate time. Table 3.14 lists the disrupters in this category.

Possible workarounds for disrupters in this category follow one or more of several general approaches. Either seek different trainees, who are not involved in ongoing operations (when the OPTEMPO is too high); work to improve the situation with the available trainees by negotiating with their commanders or providing some type of incentive for training; or adjust the training to be better suited to the availability and skills of the available trainees, which could be as easy as arranging to train in the afternoon rather than the morning or scaling back the curriculum to provide more basic training rather than advanced skills. The latter is probably the easiest (you change the training rather than the trainees) but is likely to result in overall training goals falling short (at least in the short term). Other solutions are possible, in context. For example, when interoperability between PN services was poor, one country in the Pacific Command AOR mandated joint training exercises between two different services, which functioned as a forcing mechanism to introduce each service to the culture of the other and to familiarize each with the other's tactics, techniques, and procedures.

Specific possible workarounds identified in the logic model include the following:

- Suspend activity and reengage appropriate decisionmakers.
- Contract translators with appropriate background.
- Initiate language training in country.
- Engage appropriate PN counterparts to reassign personnel.
- Modify the training plan to include an introductory section on basic skills, if practical.

Table 3.14
Disrupters: PN Personnel and Trainee

Disrupter	Input Category
PN does not provide sufficient personnel	PN personnel (trainees)
The number of trainees assigned does not account for expected attrition	PN personnel (trainees)
Insufficient language-fluent PN personnel are available	PN personnel (trainees)
Trainees do not have the prerequisite basic familiarity with equipment or assigned tasks	PN personnel (trainees)
PN personnel are not motivated to train	PN personnel (trainees)
OPTEMPO restricts time available for training	PN personnel (trainees)
Trainee attention is lacking (distracted, high, fatigued, unauthorized absence, etc.)	PN personnel (trainees)
Trainees are unable to attend due to other duty requirements	PN personnel (trainees)
Trainees lack literacy, aptitude, or physical conditioning for training	PN personnel (trainees)
PN personnel lack the capacity to learn how to use new equipment	Equipment (to be trained on)
PN personnel are not accustomed to consulting manuals and following procedures	Equipment (to be trained on)
PN personnel do not show ability or inclination to maintain living quarters, training facilities, or field areas	Facilities (including security)
Poor retention of PN personnel following training does not permit PN forces to increase force capability	PN personnel (trainees)

- Modify the training plan to conduct less training or to focus on training the trainer.
- Modify the training plan with regard to timing and classroom hours.
- Engage to have trainees assigned as a permanent change of station or to modify the training schedule to accommodate PN personnel's other obligations.
- Adjust the training program to train smaller numbers of qualified personnel.
- Modify the training plan to build initial capacity prior to introducing new equipment.
- Adjust training certification standards.
- Use U.S. service manuals as training materials.
- Contract U.S. (or third-party) personnel to conduct maintenance.
- Propose retention bonuses for trained PN personnel.

Disrupter Category: PN Infrastructure, Facilities, and Logistics

A variety of broader contextual challenges, such as a weak economy, poor governance, low military spending, or low regard for the military countrywide can result in short-comings in infrastructure, facilities, or logistics. While easy to overlook, deficiencies in this area can spoil training just as easily as too few or undermotivated trainees. Something as simple a lack of secure housing for U.S. trainers on site can result in a failed or delayed BPC effort (in one case we examined, such a lack delayed planned training delivery for more than six months). Table 3.15 lists the disrupters in this area identified in the logic model.

Table 3.15
Disrupters: PN Infrastructure, Facilities, and Logistics

Disrupter	Input Category
The infrastructure available for movement is inadequate (poor roads, etc.)	PN personnel (trainees)
Range facilities do not exist to facilitate safe firing exercises	Equipment (to be trained on)
PN logistics approval process is insufficient	Equipment (to be trained on)
PN communications are not secure	Equipment (to be trained on)
Transport resources are not available	Logistics and transport
PN lacks adequate medical capacity	Logistics and transport
Current base facilities are not adequate for quarters	Facilities (including security)
The base does not meet FP standards	Facilities (including security)
The base does not have adequate functional space (classroom, administration)	Facilities (including security)
The PN does not provide adequate supplies (training aids, smart boards or chalkboards)	Facilities (including security)
The facility does not have adequate field areas, or the field areas are in disrepair	Facilities (including security)
The PN electrical grid is inadequate, or the facility infrastructure is unable to support electrical demand	Facilities (including security)
The base equipment and infrastructure are insufficient	Facilities (including security)
PN infrastructure does not support information technology systems	Facilities (including security)

Workarounds again follow one or more of three general approaches: Either relocate to different facilities, improve existing facilities, or adjust training plans to accommodate shortcomings. Specific possible workarounds identified in the logic model include the following:

- Reconsider the training location; consider improving the surrounding infrastructure, if practical.
- Identify issues that need to be resolved prior to training.
- Institute frequency-hopping and other methods to protect unencrypted communications.
- Consider providing U.S. transport assets.
- Train medical personnel.
- Provide missing resources from U.S. sources.
- Contract to refurbish existing structures.
- Consider a change of venue or an alternative location.
- House U.S. trainers at a separate location.
- Consider providing temporary prefabricated buildings.
- Contract to prepare adequate areas.
- Provide generators.
- Contract to improve base infrastructure.
- Fund infrastructure improvements if possible; modify training curriculum to limit reliance on information technology.

Some of these could lead to further sustainment issues and so should be considered carefully.

CHAPTER FOUR

Recommendations

The findings and results from the analyses presented here and in previous RAND research in this area led us to the following recommendations.

Get Your Own House in Order

As noted, many of the contextual challenges encountered stem from or are exacerbated by shortcomings in U.S. policy or practice. Especially when working with a partner whose characteristics or behaviors contribute to contextual challenges, it is critical that U.S. contributions be well coordinated and conducted. We have four specific recommendations in this regard.

First, **BPC planners and program or resource managers should engage senior leaders and resource managers at every stage of the planning cycle, from concept to evaluation, to ensure that aspects under U.S. control are well coordinated and conducted**. Planners should earnestly commit to vigorous engagement with the bureaucracy and stakeholders to carefully stitch together the patchwork of authorities and mechanisms that exist to facilitate a cohesive and efficient BPC effort. Effective coordination may require the attention of senior leaders. This process involves both a greater understanding of the various BPC funding sources and their requirements and closer cooperation among the agencies (both military and civilian) that are engaged in BPC on a policy level and in the field. Planners and program and resource managers should attend as many focused security cooperation conferences as they can manage, since networking is critical to success with the patchwork of authorities and mechanisms. Moreover, forming and committing to regular participation in monitoring and evaluation focus groups with interagency participants to discuss ongoing BPC efforts, especially when large numbers of resources are involved, can be most useful. Second, in keeping with the recommendations of Moroney and colleagues,[1] **ask Congress to reform existing BPC mechanisms to increase responsiveness, simplify processes, promote sustainment, and strengthen spending control**. While some of the hard

---

[1] Moroney, Thaler, and Hogler, 2013.

work of aligning and coordinating U.S. efforts falls on those who plan, manage, and execute such efforts, some of the existing authorities and regulations place undue burdens on those involved in this process. For example, several existing authorities and associated resources are tied to training and equipping SOF, when perhaps they should include conventional forces; similarly, some counterterrorism authorities are limited to certain countries or regions and should perhaps be considered on a global scale. As yet another example, some funding sources cannot be mixed; currently, long-term foreign military financing cannot be used to sustain capabilities built under short-term section 1206–funded efforts. Existing mechanisms either need to be changed to allow more-durable and sustained engagement across a broader range of partners or need to be joined by (or replaced by) new ones. For example, if every section 1206 case were supported by a matched and corresponding sustainment package (either using a new authority or built using the available patchwork), capabilities built using section 1206 funds would be more likely to endure.

Third, and also requiring procedural reform, **increase options for agility available to managers and executors, both to respond to changes on the ground and to incentivize or disincentivize PN behaviors, as needed**. Errors made elsewhere in the BPC patchwork bureaucracy would be less critical if they could be corrected easily further down the chain; this is particularly true for decisions on equipment or materiel. In countries where interservice rivalries may prohibit one branch from acquiring newer or more-modern weapons, equipment, and technology instead of another, these issues should be identified *before* funding is approved for such purchases, in an effort to save time and money. Better coordination across the bureaucracy could increase agility; first, if U.S. government stakeholders are engaged at all levels of planning, senior leaders can delegate authority more easily; second, actively attending regular Office of the Secretary of Defense (OSD)–, CCMD-, and service-sponsored security cooperation conferences is one way to air and then resolve these issues. Increased funding flexibility would allow those delivering BPC to reallocate funds to solve emergent problems and save otherwise failing engagements or events. Agility with regard to the flow of delivery of BPC or funds (spigot control: on, off, open a trickle) in country would enable greater finesse in encouraging the cooperation of PN counterparts and greater selectivity in disincentivizing bad behavior (corruption, human rights abuses, etc.).

Fourth, U.S. coordination could be greatly facilitated by **better information sharing among the various agencies engaged in BPC**. Providing a forum for U.S. trainers to share insights into how to engage with partners in challenging contexts would be helpful in addressing common obstacles and developing more-effective workarounds. Trainers need to better connect to the policy community to bring issues to light. The CCMD Security Cooperation Education and Training Working Groups are one example. Forming virtual communities of interest typically works as a way to push information out to the interagency stakeholders who need to know. Improved information sharing would also be beneficial in improving the assessment of BPC efforts. Only by combining the insights of various U.S. personnel engaged with PN forces can an adequate picture be drawn of PN capabilities.

Anticipate Challenges and Plan Accordingly

The challenges and potential disrupters that can constrain BPC efforts should not come as a surprise. Those that are likely (or just possible) should be identified in planning, prepared against, and monitored in execution.

Survey likely challenges at the outset of an effort. During planning (perhaps at the CCMD or the service component command level) and also before specific BPC events (training events in particular), the likelihood of possible challenges and disrupters should be identified, assessed (perhaps holistically, using a framework like the one proposed here), and documented. Areas identified as possible trouble spots should be scrutinized with greater intensity (either additional subject-matter expert input or formal data collection).

Anticipate challenges and plan workarounds. Once likely challenges have been identified, prioritize the elimination or amelioration of those most likely to seriously disrupt the effort (the red or orange challenges). When possible, put preventative workarounds in place to decrease the likelihood of high-threat disruptions. When prevention is not feasible, plans should include branches and sequels, should possible disruptions emerge. To support such efforts, maintain constant vigilance for emergent challenges and disrupters, so that they can be fixed or worked around as soon as possible. Contingency plans should be put into place in the event the most grievous challenges are not overcome. When possible, ensure that PN officials understand that these challenges may disrupt future BPC plans.

Include assessment considerations in the planning process. Planning should include not only preliminary assessments or likely challenges but also the collection of assessment data throughout the process. Much valuable assessment information can be collected informally from U.S. trainers or other personnel in the field, but some will require more-rigorous data-collection efforts, and these assessment requirements should be identified and put in place during the planning phase. Assessments should be discussed in preengagement events and, of course, in the red team discussions postevent. Something specific that can support assessment is to stipulate assessment (and related data collection) as part of the orders and contracts involved in the execution of BPC. Further, the planning phase is an opportunity to make sure the BPC objectives are SMART. If they are not, both planning and later assessment will suffer. Finally, in challenging contexts, it is important to gather information on PN willingness to engage in BPC and PN sustainment capabilities as part of the required assessments.

Match Delivery to Partners' Willingness, Interests, and Absorption Capacity

Effective BPC matches U.S. national interests to what the partner wants and is actually capable of using. First, **strive to reach shared BPC objectives with the PN.** Having concordant objectives, documented at a level of specificity that allows collaborative planning, is important. Sharing objectives is relatively straightforward where there are substantial overlaps between U.S. and PN security interests, but where these diverge, some kind of agreement on objectives must be found. The devil is in the details, whether there is broad agreement or not. Where the United States and the PN have different priorities, some kind of compromise or quid pro quo may be required. At a minimum, U.S. officials should understand where key objectives diverge from those of the PNs, and this knowledge should be shared widely, particularly with the training teams that regularly engage the PNs. For example, if, as is often the case, the United States wants to build capacity to resolve one kind of security threat (for example, counternarcotics or border security), but the PN's threat priorities lie elsewhere (perhaps internal security or counterpiracy), it would likely be better to reach an agreement that accommodates both countries' concerns. This might include building dual-use capabilities to combat multiple types of threats—perhaps a unit that can counter narcotics trafficking (a U.S. concern) and also respond to piracy (a primary PN concern). An alternative might be an agreement to build capabilities that can be dispersed across a larger area to satisfy divergent U.S. and PN threat priorities, perhaps one trained formation established at a northern border location to address the primary U.S. concern and one in the south to address the primary PN concern. Coming to a negotiated settlement on how and where newly established capabilities will be employed will likely reduce the risk that the PN will appropriate all-new capabilities for its top priority or be less motivated to participate because the BPC does not align with the top priority.

When there are no shared interests and when some sort of compromise cannot be reached, it is important to recognize that BPC may sometimes not be the most appropriate U.S. foreign policy tool. For some challenges and in some contexts, BPC is not advisable, or its onset should be delayed until certain other developments (in terms of shared interests, willingness, or ministerial capacity) are in place.

Second, **match equipment to partners, both in terms of what they can use and what they can maintain**. Too often, equipment provided through BPC is ill suited to PN forces, either because it is too sophisticated for them, ill suited to their environment or terrain, or beyond their capability (or inclination) to maintain. Despite the preference (of the United States and PNs) to address capability gaps quickly with high-end equipment and support, a longer-term, building-block approach, tailored to a PN's existing capabilities, would work best. It is important to recognize the limits to what a PN can absorb early on and to pace BPC efforts accordingly, to ensure that U.S. equipment is used appropriately rather than relegated to a warehouse because of a lack of technical or maintenance capacity. Detailed surveys of the equipment the PNs already have; an understanding of the resources they have to operate, maintain, and sustain the equipment; and a sense of the PN politics that underpin the entire process are helpful. Make sure that equipment choices are based on what works for the PN, not what is most convenient for the United States.

Plan for Sustainment

Related to the need to match equipment to partners is the need to **plan for sustainment, which should be discussed broadly within the U.S. interagency with all key stakeholders**. A complete sustainment plan will recognize what ongoing inputs and activities will need to take place to sustain trained and equipped forces. This includes ongoing funding, refresher or extended training, replacement equipment, spare parts, maintenance skills, and maintenance activities. The sustainment plan should include details about where these inputs (especially funding) will come from and who will conduct the needed activities. This sustainment plan must be developed in concert with the PN, particularly when the expectation is that the PN will fund significant sustainment costs. Care should be taken in making assumptions about input and activities to be undertaken by the PN. PN ministerial capacity may be inadequate (or the PN military may be inadequately funded) to manage the logistics tail needed for physical sustainment. PN forces may be insufficiently equipped, insufficiently trained, or insufficiently motivated to perform needed maintenance. Absent a concerted effort to address these issues at the ministerial level through reform, a good rule of thumb is to understand the PN's sustainment limitations and consider the PN force's baseline maintenance effort for equipment that it already has, then manage expectations for what can realistically be accomplished accordingly. If the PN is not maintaining its existing equipment, do not imagine that it is likely to do any better maintaining anything the United States provides. The sustainment plan may need to treat equipment as disposable, with periodic wholesale replacement, rather than with any kind of expectation of maintenance. When possible, consider sharing the sustainment plan with the PN to increase transparency and manage expectations.

Recognizing the limited capacity of many countries in challenging contexts and the constraints on the United States to provide ongoing assistance, it is important for the United States to focus on building PN capabilities that have the greatest potential for sustainment and growth. **BPC activities that tie persistent training engagements to equipment procurement, for example, have a higher likelihood of being maintained and expanded over time.** Priority may also be given to efforts the PN is willing to devote its own resources to supporting.

In determining where to dedicate U.S. sustainment funding, it can also help to prioritize the capabilities the PN shows the greatest willingness to use and maintain.

Rather than attempting to support all U.S. BPC activities, **targeting U.S. sustainment efforts on a few capabilities that demonstrate some evidence of success will likely be more effective over the long term**.

Strive for Consistency, but Retain Agility

Struggling BPC is characterized by fits and starts, moving targets, interrupted funding and delivery, disgruntled players, and constantly changing points of contact. To the extent possible, when managing and executing BPC, **strive for consistency over time in terms of objectives, funding, and plans**. At every level of the BPC bureaucracy, envision and execute based on a cumulative, building-block approach, rather than beginning anew at each step. Minor adjustments to make something work better can preserve existing successes and build cumulatively toward reaching objectives and goals. Consistency over time requires a long-term view.

We mentioned the need for more-flexible authorities earlier, but with or without revised authorities, conducting BPC in a challenging context requires agility in planning and execution. Specifically, be willing to **work with PN elements that are willing (and able) to work with U.S. counterparts**. Especially when PN willingness is limited, working with an interested PN formation that is perhaps less aligned with core strategic goals can allow an initial success, which can create momentum and incentives for other PN units to become more cooperative. BPC can take time, and starting with a willing counterpart is more likely to contribute to long-term success. This same logic applies to contexts that include human rights constraints; working successfully with an eager partner unit that is free from human rights concerns creates incentives for other units to protect their human rights standing or to seek out and cooperate with vetting processes.

Catalog of Identified Disrupters

Table A.1 is a compilation of the disrupters discussed in the body of this report. In the table, all disrupters appeared in at least one of the four case studies unless offset in italics

Table A.1
Disrupters, by Disrupter Category

Disrupter Category and Disrupter	Logic Model Input Category
Objectives and goals	
U.S. goals are unrealistic in terms of capability improvement or time required	U.S. program goals
Attainment of standards is not likely in the time and resources allotted	Curriculum, POI, training content
Standards are not matched to baseline proficiency of PN trainees	Curriculum, POI, training content
Objectives or mission scope change	U.S. political will
Projected U.S. funds are insufficient, and funding is used up prior to completion of program	Funding
Medical personnel are not aware of training demands and disqualify trainees unnecessarily or clear them inappropriately	Logistics and transport
U.S. internal contention	
There is disagreement on PN needs for training	U.S. program goals
There is disagreement on resourcing	U.S. program goals
There is disagreement on methodology	U.S. program goals
There is disagreement on program longevity	U.S. program goals
There is disagreement over who pays	U.S. program goals
Stakeholders continue to argue for modifications to the BPC plan	U.S. program goals
The disrupter is resistance at the congressional, OSD, or CCMD level	U.S. political will
There is resistance from the in-country team (embassy or military group)	U.S. political will
Embassy officials are focused on other efforts and are not involved once training begins	U.S. political will

Table A.1—Continued

Disrupter Category and Disrupter	Logic Model Input Category
U.S. continuity and agility	
Continuity (personnel rotations, etc.) is lacking	U.S. program goals
Momentum is lost after original training event	U.S. political will
There are delays in funding or obligation of funds	Funding
In-country team cannot redirect funds when problems arise	Funding
Funds do not carry into following years	Funding
Resources are reallocated at a higher level during program	Funding
Military construction funds are not available or not permitted for training	Facilities
U.S.-PN relationships	
U.S. personnel lack understanding of PN structures and personnel	U.S. program goals
U.S. or PN facilitators deviate from agreed-to plans	U.S. program goals
Insufficient or excess U.S. personnel are assigned to cover PN interactions	U.S. program goals
U.S. is unable to reach or engage senior PN officials	U.S. program goals
U.S. approach to PN officials is coordinated poorly; officials are approached out of sequence or not by the correct U.S. stakeholder	U.S. program goals
PN officials are too quick to believe U.S. involvement is no longer required	PN political will
PN counterparts change	PN political will
There is disagreement between what the PN wants and what the U.S. thinks the PN needs	PN political will
PN leaders receive an inflated view of the new capability and increase risk-prone behavior	PN political will
Culture clashes within PN forces	PN personnel (trainees)
U.S. and PN disagree on the role of equipment in the training program	Equipment (to be trained on)
PN does not believe the equipment is necessary or appropriate to do the training	Equipment (to be trained on)
U.S. and PN disagree over measures of student competence	PN political will
U.S. and PN disagree on the utility of the instructional materials	Curriculum, POI, training content
Human rights violations and restrictions	
Activities are restricted to certain activities or interactions with specific PN entities	U.S. political will and funding
Accusations are made about additional human rights concerns or abuses	U.S. political will
Insufficient personnel who have cleared the vetting process are available	PN personnel (trainees)
Bureaucratic hurdles to vetting exist	PN personnel (trainees)

Table A.1—Continued

Disrupter Category and Disrupter	Logic Model Input Category
Equipment mismatch	
PN is limited by the types or age of its existing equipment	PN political will and equipment (to be trained on)
The equipment procured is insufficient or differs from what the in-country team requested	Equipment (to be trained on)
PN cannot provide ammunition and requires a type not in the U.S. inventory	Equipment (to be trained on)
PN cannot provide parts and requires parts not in the U.S. inventory	Equipment (to be trained on)
PN personnel are not sufficiently familiar with the equipment to conduct exercises safely	Equipment (to be trained on)
PN lacks absorptive capacity to utilize information technology systems beyond training periods	Facilities
Trainers (U.S.)	
Trainers lack sufficient subject-matter expertise (or training expertise)	U.S. trainers
Trainers are insufficiently familiar with PN languages and customs	U.S. trainers
Trainers are unfamiliar with goals and intent of the training	U.S. trainers
Trainers are not communicating with PN personnel effectively	U.S. trainers
Trainers deviate from the plan	U.S. trainers
PN trainees do not respect the trainers because of rank or civilian status	U.S. trainers
PN officials, commanders, or students do not find U.S. trainers credible or trustworthy	U.S. trainers
Curriculum and training materials	
Training is insufficient to permit intended operations or to achieve standards	PN personnel (trainees) and curriculum, POI, training content
Equipment is not part of the training curriculum	Equipment (to be trained on)
Manuals were not written in the correct language or at a level that PN personnel can understand	Equipment (to be trained on)
Manuals were not cleared through the foreign disclosure or copyright process	Equipment (to be trained on)
Curriculum does not follow a form familiar to trainees	Curriculum, POI, training content
Curriculum becomes outdated quickly	Curriculum, POI, training content
Sustainment	
PN does not agree to focus on sustainment and maintenance	PN political will
PN officials are content to permit continued U.S. handling of functions that the PN could perform	PN political will
PN does not allocate resources to continue training	PN political will

Table A.1—Continued

Disrupter Category and Disrupter	Logic Model Input Category
U.S. disagreements exist on sustainment funding	U.S. program goals and plans
Maintenance and training standards are not adhered to	PN personnel (trainees)
Third-party trainers are not able to commit to involvement in future iterations	U.S. trainers
PN personnel are unaccustomed or unwilling to perform daily maintenance actions	Equipment (to be trained on)
PN lacks appropriate personnel for maintenance	Equipment (to be trained on)
PN does not keep up preventative maintenance practices	Equipment (to be trained on)
U.S. applies a contractor support model that the PN cannot carry forward	Facilities
PN personnel and trainees	
PN does not provide sufficient personnel	PN personnel (trainees)
The number of trainees assigned does not account for expected attrition	PN personnel (trainees)
Insufficient language-fluent PN personnel are available	PN personnel (trainees)
Trainees do not have the prerequisite basic familiarity with equipment or assigned tasks	PN personnel (trainees)
PN personnel are not motivated to train	PN personnel (trainees)
OPTEMPO restricts time available for training	PN personnel (trainees)
Trainee attention is lacking (distracted, high, fatigued, unauthorized absence, etc.)	PN personnel (trainees)
Trainees are unable to attend due to other duty requirements	PN personnel (trainees)
Trainees lack literacy, aptitude, or physical conditioning for training	PN personnel (trainees)
PN personnel lack the capacity to learn how to use new equipment	Equipment (to be trained on)
PN personnel are not accustomed to consulting manuals and following procedures	Equipment (to be trained on)
PN personnel do not show the ability or inclination to maintain living quarters, training facilities, or field areas	Facilities
Poor retention of PN personnel following training does not permit PN forces to increase force capability	PN personnel (trainees)
PN infrastructure, facilities, and logistics	
The infrastructure available for movement is inadequate (poor roads, etc.)	PN personnel (trainees)
Range facilities sufficient for safe firing exercises are unavailable	Equipment (to be trained on)

Table A.1—Continued

Disrupter Category and Disrupter	Logic Model Input Category
PN logistics approval process is insufficient	Equipment (to be trained on)
PN communications are not secure	Equipment (to be trained on)
Transport resources are not available	Logistics and transport
PN lacks adequate medical capacity	Logistics and transport
Current base facilities are not adequate for quarters	Facilities
The base does not meet FP standards	Facilities
The base does not have adequate functional space (classrooms, administration)	Facilities
PN does not provide adequate supplies (training aids, smart boards or chalkboards)	Facilities
The facility does not have adequate field areas, or the field areas are in disrepair	Facilities
The PN electrical grid is inadequate, or the facility infrastructure is unable to support the electrical demand	Facilities
Base equipment and infrastructure are insufficient	Facilities
PN infrastructure does not support information technology systems	Facilities
PN willingness to support and conduct BPC	
PN is afraid that U.S. assistance will unbalance internal power dynamics and so is resistant	PN political will
PN support is lacking because of honest misunderstanding or translation issues	PN political will
PN government and ministerial support are not communicated to or not shared by frontline units and personnel	PN political will
PN officials are focused on other efforts and are not involved once training begins	PN political will
PN does not fund transfer of personnel	PN personnel (trainees)
PN slow-rolls process or assigns inferior personnel to the program	PN personnel (trainees)
PN trainees are not assigned in a timely manner	PN personnel (trainees)
PN is reluctant to "waste" equipment operations on training	Equipment (to be trained on)
Transport resources are utilized for other purposes or missions	Logistics and transport
Authorities are not established for release of parts and fuel	Logistics and transport
PN is reluctant to provide access to examine facilities	Facilities
PN officials are reluctant to have U.S. personnel living near the training facility	Facilities

Table A.1—Continued

Disrupter Category and Disrupter	Logic Model Input Category
PN will not permit changes or procedures that would conform with FP requirements	Facilities
PN is unwilling or unable to provide facility staff	Facilities
PN willingness to organize for increased capacity	
PN shows no interest or ability in sustaining program results	U.S. program goals
PN supports BPC efforts but does not prioritize the mission that BPC is intended to enhance	PN political will
There is no indication that PN officials plan to change operations or use trainees as intended (or according to U.S. objectives)	PN political will
Trained personnel are not used as intended (not assigned to take advantage of training received)	PN personnel (trainees)
PN creates temporary composite units to receive training and equipment (and spread resources across PN stakeholders), then disbands the units	PN personnel (trainees)
PN personnel are not allowed to utilize new equipment after completion of training	Equipment (to be trained on)
PN personnel do not choose to use new equipment after completion of training	Equipment (to be trained on)
PN policy does not permit deployment for international operations	Curriculum, POI, training content
Corruption or governance	
Corruption diverts funding or other resources	Funding
Unequal pay compared to other PN services	PN personnel (trainees)
PN does not release or diverts equipment prior to training	Equipment (to be trained on)
Ammunition is diverted from training, or PN personnel sell ammunition	Equipment (to be trained on)
Equipment is diverted posttraining	Equipment (to be trained on)
PN does not establish part-release procedures or loses parts to corruption	Equipment (to be trained on)
Disbursing funds is difficult in country	Funding
Delivery of material is delayed or impeded by customs or bureaucracy	Logistics and transport
PN corruption leads to poor fuel quality	Logistics and transport
PN laws do not support the U.S. training mission and the status of U.S. trainers sufficiently	Logistics and transport
PN funds are exhausted or halted due to instability or other reasons beyond counterparts' control	Funding
Security situation	
It is difficult to move U.S. trainers safely to the training facility	Logistics and transport

Table A.1—Continued

Disrupter Category and Disrupter	Logic Model Input Category
Extracting U.S. trainers in the event of natural disaster, security breach, etc., is challenging	Logistics and transport
Training conditions necessitate housing U.S. personnel at separate location	Facilities
FP requirements cannot be met	Facilities
PN modifies facilities after U.S. departure so that they are no longer FP compliant	Facilities

References

Bailey, John J., and Roy Godson, *Organized Crime and Democratic Governability: Mexico and the U.S.-Mexican Borderlands*, Pittsburgh, Pa.: University of Pittsburgh Press, 2001.

Felbab-Brown, Vanda, *Shooting Up: Counterinsurgency and the War on Drugs*, Washington, D.C.: Brookings Institution Press, 2009.

Joint Publication 3-0, *Joint Operations*, Washington, D.C.: U.S. Department of Defense, August 11, 2011.

Jones, Seth G., Olga Oliker, Peter Chalk, C. Christine Fair, Rollie Lal, and James Dobbins, *Securing Tyrants or Fostering Reform? U.S. Internal Security Assistance to Repressive and Transitioning Regimes*, Santa Monica, Calif.: RAND Corporation, MG-550-OSI, 2006. As of December 9, 2014: http://www.rand.org/pubs/monographs/MG550.html

Mathis, James J., "Solving Colombia's Problems," Carlisle, Pa.: U.S. Army War College, 2003.

McNerney, Michael J., Jennifer D. P. Moroney, Peter Mandaville, and Terry Hagen, *New Security and Justice Sector Partnership Models: Implications of the Arab Uprisings*, Santa Monica, Calif.: RAND Corporation, RR-605-DOS, 2014. As of December 9, 2014: http://www.rand.org/pubs/research_reports/RR605.html

Mertens, Donna M., and Amy T. Wilson, *Program Evaluation Theory and Practice: A Comprehensive Guide*, New York: The Guilford Press, 2012.

Moroney, Jennifer D. P., Beth Grill, Joe Hogler, Lianne Kennedy Boudali, and Christopher Paul, *How Successful Are U.S. Efforts to Build Capacity in Developing Countries? A Framework to Assess the Global Train and Equip "1206" Program*, Santa Monica, Calif.: RAND Corporation, TR-1121-OSD, 2011. As of December 9, 2014: http://www.rand.org/pubs/technical_reports/TR1121.html

Moroney, Jennifer D. P., David E. Thaler, and Joe Hogler, *Review of Security Cooperation Mechanisms Combatant Commands Utilize to Build Partner Capacity*, Santa Monica, Calif.: RAND Corporation, RR-413-OSD, 2013. As of December 9, 2014: http://www.rand.org/pubs/research_reports/RR413.html

National Security Presidential Directive 18, "Supporting Policy in Columbia," Washington, D.C.: The White House, November 2002.

Office of the Special Inspector General for Afghanistan Reconstruction, "Actions Needed to Improve the Reliability of Afghan Security Force Assessments," June 29, 2010.

Paul, Christopher, Colin P. Clarke, Beth Grill, Stephanie Young, Jennifer D. P. Moroney, Joe Hogler, and Christine Leah, *What Works Best When Building Partner Capacity and Under What Circumstances?* Santa Monica, Calif.: RAND Corporation, MG-1253/1-OSD, 2013. As of December 9, 2014: http://www.rand.org/pubs/monographs/MG1253z1.html

Paul, Christopher, Brian Gordon, Jennifer D. P. Moroney, Lisa Saum-Manning, Beth Grill, Colin P. Clarke, and Heather Peterson, *A Building Partner Capacity Assessment Framework: Tracking Inputs, Outputs, Outcomes, Disrupters, and Workarounds*, Santa Monica, Calif.: RAND Corporation, RR-935-OSD, 2015.

Paul, Christopher, Michael Nixon, Heather Peterson, Beth Grill, and Jessica Yeats, *The RAND Security Cooperation Prioritization and Propensity Matching Tool*, Santa Monica, Calif.: RAND Corporation, TL-112-OSD, 2013. As of December 9, 2014:
http://www.rand.org/pubs/tools/TL112.html

Paul, Christopher, Jessica M. Yeats, Colin P. Clarke, and Miriam Mathews, *Assessing and Evaluating Efforts to Inform, Influence, and Persuade: Desk Reference*, Santa Monica, Calif.: RAND Corporation, RR-809/1-OSD, 2015.

Rossi, Peter H., Mark W. Lipsey, and Howard E. Freeman, *Evaluation: A Systematic Approach*, Thousand Oaks, Calif.: Sage Publications, 2004.

"Senate Moves Toward Supporting U.S. Helicopters for Iraq," Reuters, January 9, 2014.

Spencer, David E., Carlos O. Ospina, David R. Moreno, Alejandro Arbelaez, Juan Carlos Gomez, Carlos Berrios, and Jorge L. Vargas, "Colombia's Road to Recovery: Security and Governance 1982–2010," National Defense University, Center for Hemispheric Defense Studies, 2011.

"UK Military Trainers in Pakistan Are Withdrawn," BBC, June 27, 2011.

White House, Office of the Press Secretary, "Fact Sheet: U.S. Security Sector Assistance Policy," April 5, 2013.